Bringing Home the Missing Linck is a compelling testimony to the grace and provision of our Lord, no matter what our circumstances. Jennifer writes with passion, emotion, and honesty as she recounts their adoption journey, clearly revealing God's undeniable hand at work along the way. Their story is an encouragement for every believer, especially those walking through a season of waiting and heartache. This is a moving testimony, a call to rise up for the cause of the orphan, and a challenge to embrace whatever road God has laid before us. *Bringing Home the Missing Linck* is a must-read for moms everywhere.

KAYSE PRATT,
writer at www.kaysepratt.com

In *Bringing Home the Missing Linck: A Journey of Faith to Family*, you'll hear the heart of a woman who is closely connected to her heavenly Father and who trusted Him to make her a mom. Jennifer candidly shares her struggles through infertility, serving in a homeless mission, and finally sitting alongside a birth mom in a hospital delivery room. Her story of becoming a mom has both pain and joy. As you read it, you'll find yourself trusting God for your own circumstances and resting in His faithfulness.

SHELLY ROBERTS,
author of *31 Nuggets of Hope:*
For Moms Who Said Yes to the Fatherless

D1407023

Jennifer Linck has captured her family's adoption journey in a transparent and God-honoring way. An interesting read, it allows the reader to grow in knowledge of the world of adoption, the joy and the pain. Thank you for your honest portrayal of God's work in your life for orphaned and vulnerable children.

KIM DE BLECOURT,
author of *Until We All Come Home*

Bringing Home the Missing Linck is a beautiful illustration of how adoption is as much a spiritual journey as it is a physical one. Jennifer writes with beautiful honesty about infertility and the unexpected and twisting path God took them on to find their Missing Linck.

JULIE GUMM,
author of *Adopt without Debt:*
Creative Ways to Cover the Cost of Adoption

Bringing Home *the* Missing Linck

A Journey of Faith to Family

JENNIFER JACKSON LINCK

WestBow
PRESS
A DIVISION OF THOMAS NELSON

WestBow Press books may be ordered through booksellers or by contacting:

WestBow Press
A Division of Thomas Nelson
1663 Liberty Drive
Bloomington, IN 47403
www.westbowpress.com
1 (866) 928-1240

Because of the dynamic nature of the Internet, any web addresses or
links contained in this book may have changed since publication and
may no longer be valid. The views expressed in this work are solely those
of the author and do not necessarily reflect the views of the publisher,
and the publisher hereby disclaims any responsibility for them.

Certain stock imagery © Thinkstock.
Any people depicted in stock imagery provided by Thinkstock are
models, and such images are being used for illustrative purposes only.

All Scripture quotations, unless otherwise indicated, are taken from the *Holy
Bible, New International Version*®. Copyright © 1973, 1978, 1984 by International
Bible Society. Used by permission of Zondervan. All rights reserved.

ISBN: 978-1-4908-1235-9 (e)
ISBN: 978-1-4908-1236-6 (sc)
ISBN: 978-1-4908-1237-3 (hc)

Library of Congress Control Number: 2013918557

Printed in the United States of America.

WestBow Press rev. date: 10/24/2013

For Jackson Henry
I loved you the moment God placed adoption on my heart.
I am so glad He chose me to be your mommy.

A plan of profound importance exists that
sometimes overrides the miracle we desperately desire.
—Beth Moore, *Jesus, the One and Only*

FOREWORD

Chosen. I grew up hearing that word. I grew up believing that word. I grew up holding to that word. Most of us know what it is to be chosen, or even *not* to be chosen. On the playground, two team captains choose their teams. Everyone holds his or her breath. "I pick you," and you hope you hear your name. You feel a loyalty to that team and that captain because he or she chose you. You run fast. You catch the ball. You try your best because he or she picked you.

My parents picked me. I grew up hearing our story. I grew up knowing they had made a choice. Their choice involved faith. They trusted God for the path He was leading them down. This path had not been traveled by others in the family, nor by any of their friends. They were the first. It was new, unexplored, not the norm. It was part of their faith journey.

Beloved. I grew up hearing that word. My parents choose to speak this word to me. Neither of them grew up in a home where that word was spoken often. They said they knew, but they were just not told. It is important to hear. Jesus Himself heard this at His baptism. "No sooner had Jesus come up out of the water than He saw the heavens torn apart and the Spirit, like a dove, descending on Him. And a voice came from heaven: 'You are my Son, the Beloved, my favor rests on you." (Matthew 3:16–17). This was placed in my head and in my heart. And I believed it.

Adopted. I grew up hearing that word. I really did not know many others who were adopted. I knew that my situation was different from most others. Different is not a bad thing, just different. When I responded to the good news of the gospel, I heard those words again: *chosen, beloved, adopted.* "For He chose us in Him before the creation of the world to be holy and blameless. In love He predestined us to be adopted as His sons through Jesus Christ, in accordance with His pleasure and will to the praise of His glorious grace, which He has freely given us in the One He loves" (Ephesians 1:4–6).

Jennifer and John chose to follow God down this path. When I heard their story, I knew it needed to be told. Their journey was the path of choosing. Their journey was the path of the beloved. Their journey was the path of adoption. They encountered many people on their path—some supportive, some not, some not sure. They had ups and downs, mountaintops and valleys. But every step of the way was God. And there was Jackson. He is chosen. He is beloved. He is adopted. They are family.

Their path had turns and obstacles, doubts and fears. Their path had joy, victory, and faith. I pray as you join them on this path through the pages of this book that God will encourage and bless you. God is still God. He is still on His throne. He still works and blesses and creates. He still makes families.

Jesus said, "As you have done it unto the least of these, you have done it unto me" (Matthew 25:40).

—Werth Mayes, pastor of Cowboy Church of Erath County

ACKNOWLEDGMENTS

I said I'd never write a book, yet here I am, trying to find the words to express my gratitude to each person who made this dream possible.

This story is not mine; it's His. To my Savior Jesus, who gave me a passion for writing and has entrusted me with a story that oftentimes I don't feel I deserve. My prayers were answered "far more than [I] could have imagined, guessed, or requested in my wildest dreams" (Ephesians 3:20).

John, I love you. I can't imagine being on this incredible journey with anyone else. It hasn't always been easy, but I wouldn't change a thing. Thank you for being a single dad on the weekends so I could write. Thank you for believing in me even though it's not likely I'll become a best-selling author and make enough money for you to quit your job. Sorry to disappoint you.

To Jackson's Pop, Lolli, Auntie M, Uncle Paulie, Dude, Missy, Aunt Adrienne, and Uncle Scott—thank you for your love and support as we waited to bring our Missing Linck home.

Dad and Mom, seeing how much you love Jackson fills my heart with joy. I've watched God do so much through this little boy, not just in my life but also in and through both of you. Thank you for all the nights you stayed up with him and told John and I to go to bed. I love you both.

Mom, you are one of the strongest people I know. You faced a tough battle, but you conquered cancer with courage. Not many people would travel four hours to their daughter's baby shower two weeks after surgery or stay up with a colicky baby after chemo, but you did. I'm amazed at the timing of Jackson's arrival. I don't think it's a coincidence. God knew you would need Jackson when the cancer seemed all-consuming, and He knew Jackson needed you to be his Lolli.

To A—Thank you will never seem adequate for the gift you have given me. You will always hold a special place in my heart. "I thank my God every time I remember you … being confident that He who began a good work in you will carry it on to completion until the day of Christ Jesus" (Philippians 1:3, 6).

To Justin and Jessica—We cherish your friendship. Thank you for walking this journey with us. Thank you for keeping us sane when we thought the screaming would never end. Thank you for loving Jackson so much.

To Amber—"Some people come into our lives and quickly go. Some stay for a while, leave footprints on our hearts, and we are never, ever the same" (Flavia Weedn). Your friendship is irreplaceable. I couldn't have finished this book without your prayers, love, and support. I lost count of the times I called you discouraged. Thank you for pushing me to finish and believing in me when I didn't believe in myself.

To Jack—I'm a better writer because of you. Thank you for reading every word of this book, editing it, and offering feedback. I know you must have been tired of adding and deleting commas.

To Werth—God kept nudging me to call you, and I'm so glad I finally listened to Him. Thank you for allowing me to share our story with your congregation and for contributing to this book. I pray that Jackson, like you, grows up always knowing he is loved and chosen not just by his parents but by his heavenly Father too.

To each person who prayed, donated, and supported us on our journey—You each played an intricate part in uniting our Forever Family.

INTRODUCTION

This book is about more than a baby. God wanted to do more in me than merely grant my deepest desire to be a mother. The purpose of our adoption goes beyond motherhood. God weaved the lives of two ordinary people together so a baby boy could have a family and a chance at life—all to fulfill His amazing plan.

Our adoption journey was about obedience to God. When God called us to adopt a child from Ethiopia, we stepped out in faith, followed His call, and opened our hearts to a child in need of a family, love, security, and hope. I am humbled that God chose John and me for such a journey. At first, I didn't realize the extent of the journey. There were many twists and turns along the way, but it became clear that our adoption had more than an earthly purpose. God's eternal purposes were at work too. As Christians, we are called to "love the least of these" (Matthew 25:40). God's Word says, "Religion that God our Father accepts as pure and faultless is this: to look after the orphans and widows in their distress" (James 1:27).

Yes, I desperately desired to be a mother, but more than that, my heart's desire was to be obedient to God and fulfill His plan for my life. I had so many ideas of what my life was supposed to look like. I thought I would get married, have babies, and live happily ever after, but God had other plans. I never doubted God's ability to give me the desires of my heart, but that didn't make the journey to motherhood any less difficult. My desire to be a mom was God-given, and I believed He would bless me with a child. It just had to be in His perfect time and in His perfect way. I never pictured myself becoming a mother through adoption, but sometimes God takes us on a path that we would have never chosen for ourselves.

When God was leading the Israelites out of Egypt into the Promised Land, the Bible says, "God did not lead them on the road through Philistine country, though that was shorter. God said, 'If they face war, they might change their minds and return to Egypt'" (Exodus 13:17–18). As John and I waited to become parents, God taught me that, although His way might take longer, His way is always better and in our best interest. God doesn't want what's *okay* for us. He wants His *perfect* will for us. As we faced infertility and the long road to adoption, I knew I wanted the land God had promised, even if I had to take a longer, more difficult road.

As John and I wandered in our own desert, we gradually became more and more like Jesus. We waited, confident that God would reveal His plans for our family. Our relationship with Him grew deeper and more meaningful. We discovered that God's purpose for our journey was simple—that He be glorified.

This is our story, but it is only a glimpse of the miracles God worked on behalf of our family. There are many parts of the story I have chosen not to include in this book, as that is my son's story to share if he chooses to do so someday. Some of the names have been changed out of respect for and to protect individuals who were part of our journey.

CHAPTER 1

A Missing Linck

For I know the plans I have for you," declares the
LORD. "Plans to prosper you and not to harm you,
plans to give you hope and a future. Then you will
call upon me and I will listen to you. You will
seek me and find me when you seek me with all
your heart.
—JEREMIAH 29:11–13

My earliest childhood memories include Cabbage Patch
dolls and a white wooden cradle. I've wanted to be
a mom since I was five years old. As a little girl, I
dreamed of getting married and having babies.

When John and I were engaged, I swore to him that I didn't
want to start a family until I was thirty years old. We would have
four years of newlywed bliss before having children. John didn't
buy into my plan. He knew the baby bug would hit long before
I celebrated my thirtieth birthday.

We had barely finished celebrating our one-year wedding
anniversary when my biological clock began ticking like a
time bomb. John wasn't surprised when pink and blue began to
consume my thoughts.

I wanted a baby yesterday! There was just one problem. John was taking medication for his Crohn's disease, and the side effects included possible birth defects in children who were conceived while on the drug. John's doctor wasn't ready to take him off the medication and warned us that we should wait at least six weeks once John stopped taking it before trying to conceive a baby. I was frustrated, but God reminded me that I would have a child in His time.

<hr />

In January of 2010, I paced the floor, praying a plus sign would appear on the home pregnancy test lying on the bathroom counter. After the longest two minutes of my life, I reluctantly checked the test.

I willed myself not to cry when I saw that only one pink line had appeared, meaning that I was not pregnant. I chucked the test in the trash and forced myself to go on with my day, not allowing the test results to get me down. For months, I had been consumed with baby fever, and for months, my body had been playing cruel tricks on me. It was ironic how I had always feared childbirth until the plus signs weren't appearing on the pregnancy tests. Fear was exchanged for sadness and an unbearable longing to be a mother.

As I stared at negative pregnancy tests month after month, more and more of my friends shared that they were expecting tiny bundles of joy. With each announcement, my heart yearned for a child even more.

Everywhere I turned there were babies. One day, on a trip to Walmart to buy yet another pregnancy test, I felt the nasty sting of jealousy. A young mother was shopping with her three children and was obviously expecting another baby any day. She seemed impatient and bothered by the chattering little ones in her shopping cart.

I just didn't understand. Why was it so easy for some people to have children and so difficult for others? As I made my way to the register to make my purchase, I silently prayed, *I just want one, God.*

When my mind was fogged with pink and blue, I drew comfort from the women in the Bible who had also experienced baby fever. God had promised Abraham that he would be a father. Abraham endured during the long wait, but his wife Sarah became so desperate to have a child that she decided to take matters into her own hands. She forced Hagar to sleep with Abraham so she could have the child she so deeply desired (Genesis 16).

But Sarah's impatience created a bunch of unnecessary baggage (or luggage, as my mom would say). God's plan had been to bless Abraham and Sarah with a child all along; it just didn't happen as quickly as Sarah had hoped (Genesis 21). In her bible study, *No Other Gods: Confronting our Modern-Day Idols,* Kelly Minter wrote, "God had a beautiful plan for Sarah in spite of how bleak things looked. Definitely she was in a bind. She had a genuine cause for concern. But that's always going to be the place where our faith is tested. If it all looks easy and doable, it doesn't require faith."[1]

I didn't want to be like Sarah and take matters into my own hands. I wanted to be like Hannah, who chose to trust God and wait for a child. The Lord had closed Hannah's womb, but in the midst of her pain, she didn't try to fix things. She chose to run to God instead. "I was pouring out my soul to the LORD ... I have been praying here out of great anguish and grief" (1 Samuel 1:15–16). The Lord heard Hannah's heartfelt prayers and eventually blessed her with a son, whom she named Samuel because she had asked the Lord for him (1 Samuel 1:20).

When I was tempted to let baby fever get the best of me,

when I thought I couldn't handle hearing one more pregnancy announcement, I prayed I would follow in Hannah's footsteps.

I regularly ran to God and poured out my heart—the good, the bad, and the ugly that comes with infertility.

God taught me that there are times when He purposefully brings pain and hard times into our lives so we will cling to Him. God used my infertility to test my faith. Would I seek Him or other worldly things in my time of pain? Would I trust Him to give me a child in His perfect time?

As Hannah grieved her inability to conceive a child, God saw her and understood her pain. Although Hannah trusted God, she still grieved that she was barren. In my moments of pure anguish and grief, I found so much comfort in knowing that God understood my pain. Grieving and approaching God's throne of grace with pure honesty and raw emotion was okay as long as I trusted Him. Minter wrote, "The one thing we can always hold onto is that though He brings pain, it is always for our good … God has brought pain in my life but as I have surrendered to it, He has used the flames of hurt to burn away the parts that need not linger."[2]

If it had been easy for Hannah to get pregnant, she wouldn't have had the chance to experience God in such an intimate way. Like Hannah, my infertility drove me to my knees before the Lord. I began praying in a way I had never prayed before and trusting God in a way I had never trusted. As a result, my faith become stronger and I cherished my relationship with Him more than I ever had before.

I have always hated going to the doctor. The mere thought of being poked with a needle sends me into a panicked frenzy.

As I sat in the doctor's office on my twenty-eighth birthday, the same feelings from my childhood plagued me. My stomach was in knots and my heart raced as I anticipated what the doctor was going to say or do to me. John didn't realize the extent of my doctor-induced anxiety until that day. He did his best to calm my fears as we filled out paperwork and waited to be called back to an exam room.

I had scheduled the appointment so we could talk to the doctor about our desire to have a baby—but more importantly, I was curious why I hadn't had a period in several months. I was in tears by the time the nurse called me back, nervous and unsure if I wanted to hear what the doctor had to say. The appointment remains a blur, but it was the beginning of many months of testing to try to determine why my body was so out of whack.

The doctor immediately put me on medication that forced my body to have a period. Once I had a normal cycle, I would have blood taken on specific days to test my hormone levels, which would hopefully determine what was going on with my body. I went through this routine month after month, trying to determine why I was unable to conceive.

Consumed with guilt, I questioned if my past choices were to blame for my inability to have a baby. Satan loved messing with me. He whispered lies like "What's wrong with you that you can't get pregnant? Why is it so easy for everyone else? You must be paying for your past sins." Had my hope not been in Christ, I would have fallen into a pit of despair each time Satan attacked. The baby boom among my friends was tough, especially when John and I longed for a family. But even in the darkest moments, I refused to question God. I was not going to fall into Satan's trap.

One Sunday, our preacher spoke on hope in the midst of suffering and encouraged us to exude hope into the lives of others.

I prayed that my hope in God would never be overshadowed by infertility or the doubts Satan was desperate for me to believe.

I wanted to be real with people. I wasn't going to pretend that the road we were traveling was smooth. It wasn't. Some days we hit one pothole after another. The journey was filled with tears, too many doctor appointments, and a lot of unknowns and heartache, but there was always hope.

The reason for my hope is my personal relationship with Jesus Christ (1 Peter 3:15). During those difficult days, I tucked His promises in my heart and used them as weapons against Satan's schemes. Despite the hard times and the things I didn't understand, I had hope! God gave me the following beautiful and encouraging promises in the midst of one of the most difficult times of my life:

> And we know that in all things God works for the good of those who love Him, who have been called according to His purpose. (Romans 8:28)

> For I know the plans I have for you … plans to prosper you and not to harm you. Plans to give you hope and a future. (Jeremiah 29:11)

I have always felt the steadfast love of Christ and trusted that each and every detail was in the palm of His hand. That belief was the only reason I could get out of bed some days. I wanted to exude hope into the lives of others and "be prepared to give an answer to everyone who asked me to give the reason for the hope that I had" (1 Peter 3:15).

After several medical tests, I had high hopes that my doctor would put me on progesterone and then my fertility problems would be solved. I was disappointed when she told me that progesterone wouldn't do the trick. She recommended that I take Clomid, a fertility drug that would cause my body to ovulate at the proper time.

I left the doctor's office feeling very hesitant about using Clomid. In a way, I felt that using a fertility drug was playing God, and I didn't want to take matters into my own hands as Sarah had. John and I wanted a baby, but we definitely didn't want a litter of babies, and I feared that taking the drug would result in multiple pregnancies. I shared my concerns with my doctor.

"Twins are common, but triplets and quadruplets are rare," my doctor said. "I will monitor your ovaries each month to make sure you aren't at risk of having more than two babies."

After a lot of prayer, seeking advice from close friends, and researching Clomid, I realized that God had created doctors and medicine for a reason. If I had been diagnosed with cancer, I would have done chemotherapy. For some reason, my body needed medicine to ovulate at the proper time, so I decided to give Clomid a try.

When I went to have the prescription for Clomid filled, the pharmacist asked to speak to me. He seemed very concerned.

"Are you pregnant or trying to get pregnant?" he asked. I must have looked at him like he had a third eye.

"Yes," I said sarcastically while grabbing the medicine and trying to contain my laughter. Why else would I be getting a prescription for a fertility drug? But when I got in the car, I read the warnings and side effects of Clomid and immediately began second-guessing my decision. Did I want to risk visual impairment and multiple pregnancies? Several people had told me horror stories about the reactions they had while on the drug.

Thankfully, I didn't have any of the side effects that I feared, but I also didn't ovulate, which was the whole purpose for taking the medicine. With each home ovulation test, I crossed my fingers that a smiley face would appear, signifying ovulation. But each time I came up empty-handed.

A few weeks after taking the Clomid, I was scheduled to have a sonogram. My doctor noticed that my ovaries were covered with tiny cysts. Putting all my symptoms together, she finally came up with a diagnosis: polycystic ovarian syndrome (PCOS).

According to the Mayo Clinic, PCOS is the most common hormonal disorder among women of reproductive age and may become apparent following weight gain or difficulty becoming pregnant. Women with polycystic ovarian syndrome may have trouble becoming pregnant due to infrequent or lack of ovulation. Early diagnosis and treatment can help reduce the risk of long-term complications, such as type 2 diabetes, heart disease, and stroke.

I had almost all the symptoms:

- menstrual abnormality
- elevated levels of male hormones that result in physical signs, such as excess facial and body hair and adult acne. For the first time in my life, I had to wax my lip and my face was broken out like a teenager going through puberty.
- polycystic ovaries
- infertility
- obesity. I was not obese, but I had gained about twenty pounds over the course of a year.

- depression. There were days when I felt really down; days when all I did was cry. It's hard to find adequate words to describe how I felt on those days. I knew the culprit was my out-of-whack hormones because I wasn't typically a depressed or sad person. My emotions were a constant battle. For several weeks, I spent almost every lunch break crying in my car. I would get so mad at myself for not being able to snap out of the funk I was in. Many days, I just wanted to crawl in bed and pull the covers over my head.

After four months of being poked and prodded, I was relieved to finally have a diagnosis, but finding out I had PCOS stung. It had wreaked havoc on my body and caused all kinds of complications.

The doctor immediately put me on medicine that I took twice a day. She said if I wanted to conceive, I would most likely need the help of a fertility drug like Clomid, and if I did get pregnant, I would have to take another drug called metphormine in order to sustain the pregnancy.

The day I received the diagnosis, I went home and crawled under the covers. I didn't even call John to tell him what the doctor had said. I was sad and felt alone. I didn't think anyone would understand what I was going through.

After spending a few days crying and grumbling about my diagnoses, I came across 2 Corinthians 1:8–9 that says, "We were under great pressure, far beyond our ability to endure, so that we despaired of life itself. Indeed, we felt we had received the sentence of death. But this happened that we might not rely on ourselves but on God, who raises the dead."

As I tried to accept my infertility, I had to stop relying on my own strength and rely on God's. He could handle my diagnosis. God, who raised people from the dead, could open my womb if He chose to do so. He had opened Rachel's, Hannah's, Leah's, and Elizabeth's. God had also chosen to give Ruth a child when she married Boaz, although she was unable to conceive with her first husband, Mahlon. The question was, Would He open my womb? I wasn't sure, but I knew His plan was better than mine and trusted His will for my life. I was still saddened by my diagnosis, but when I felt weary and burdened and all I could do was cry, the Lord gave me rest.

I began relating to Paul. He had a thorn in his side and begged God to remove it, yet it remained. It was a constant reminder that God's grace was all Paul needed.

> My grace is sufficient for you, for my power is made perfect in weakness. Therefore I will boast all the more gladly about my weaknesses, so that Christ's power may rest on me. That is why, for Christ's sake, I delight in weaknesses, in insults, in hardships, in persecutions, in difficulties. For when I am weak, then I am strong. (2 Corinthians 12:9–10)

After a lot of prayer and through Kelly Minter's Bible study on Ruth, I felt the Lord was asking me to rest in Him and wait to have a child. Minter's words spoke to my heart and affirmed what I felt God was asking me to do. She wrote,

God requires different things at different times
during our seasons of waiting. Sometimes in our
seasons of waiting we are told to cease worrying
and tossing, quietly lean on our Savior, and rest.
Other times we are to actively wait by persisting
in praying and staying keenly alert to our
surroundings, ready for whatever appears next.
We are always to stay close to our Redeemer.[3]

The Holy Spirit was telling me to give my body a break and
to focus on my health issues. I didn't need to be in a rush. I had
plenty of time to become a mother.

I had no desire to do fertility treatments in hopes of getting
pregnant. John and I scheduled an appointment with my doctor to
discuss my PCOS and depression. I was thankful to have a doctor
who understood exactly what I was going through, as she, too,
had also faced the heartache of infertility. She didn't look at me
like I was crazy when I sat in her office and sobbed uncontrollably
for reasons I couldn't explain.

Before talking about my health problems from a professional
perspective, she stepped out of her role as my doctor and gave
me advice as someone who had been in my shoes. "Stop going
to baby showers," she said. "Go out and buy several gift cards to
Baby Gap, and send those to friends instead of attending the actual
shower. Emotionally, it will be the best decision you'll make."

After sharing her personal advice, she reassured me, from a
medical standpoint, that my emotions were warranted. Being
diagnosed with PCOS was hard enough, but the emotions
associated with infertility made it ten times worse. No wonder
I was a basket case. The doctor decided to put me back on birth
control pills in hopes that they would regulate my crazy hormones,
which would in turn would help my depression.

Although we weren't *technically* trying to get pregnant, taking birth control felt like we were taking a huge step backward. Even though I knew my body wasn't working properly and there was little chance of my getting pregnant, there was always a slight glimmer of hope that one month a plus sign would appear on a pregnancy test. That slight glimmer of hope was snuffed out once I started taking the pill.

"God, please help me trust You and Your perfect plan for my life," I prayed through tears. "I know you see my heart. I know you understand how much I want to be a mother. I know you feel my pain. Help me remember that Your plan and timing is far better than any plans I could have for myself. Please give me patience. Help me to trust You." God "heard my prayers and saw my tears" (Isaiah 38:5) and began answering that simple prayer like His Word promises in Jeremiah 33:3, "Call to me and I will answer you and tell you great and unsearchable things you do not know."

God slowly took away any desire I had to be pregnant. Being pregnant, morning sickness, and epidurals had never really appealed to me. Honestly, they scared me to death! I began realizing that my heart's desire was never to be pregnant but simply to be a mother.

One week after uttering that heartfelt prayer and releasing my desire to become a mom to the Lord, He began placing adoption on my heart.

CHAPTER 2

147 Million Orphans

I will not leave you as orphans; I will come to you.
—JOHN 14:18

A week after I had my heart-to-heart with God, we were sitting in a Mexican restaurant with our small group. As I savored chips and salsa, the Holy Spirit nudged me toward adoption for the first time.

A few weeks before, on January 12, 2010, an earthquake measuring 7.0 on the Richter scale had devastated Haiti. Before the earthquake, UNICEF estimated that there were 380,000 Haitian orphans. Determining the exact number of orphans from the earthquake that wreaked havoc on the country was impossible.

As we talked about the earthquake and the growing orphan crisis in Haiti, someone mentioned that the Haitian government was considering easing the restrictions on adoption. "John and I talked about adopting when we were dating," I told the group. "We just assumed it would happen when we were older and could afford it."

Sharing our desire to adopt started a wildfire of conversation at our table. "You and John should adopt from Haiti," Shelli said. "We'll help you raise money." Plans for a baby shower soon followed as the group contemplated how quickly John and I could board a plane to Haiti.

At that moment, God began confirming His plans for John and me to adopt. As I sat listening to the excitement buzzing at our table, chill bumps covered my body and tears filled my eyes. For the rest of the night, I sat in a fog, oblivious to what was going on around me. My food became cold and remained untouched as I thought about John and I boarding a plane, going to Haiti, and becoming a family. I have no doubt that the Holy Spirit moved that night and began softening my heart toward adoption.

As John and I drove home from dinner, our excitement grew. "What just happened?" I asked.

"I would hop on a plane to Haiti right now if I could," John said.

Anticipation bubbled up inside me over the next few days as I thought about adopting a baby. I spent a lot of time praying, asking God if adoption was really the path He wanted us to take.

I felt He answered my prayers a few days later when the Holy Spirit impressed upon my heart that adopting a baby was about more than becoming a family. God showed me that I had the opportunity to give a child a home, love, hope, security, and a future. He was giving me the chance to be His hands and feet and wanted me to open my heart to "one of the least of these" (Matthew 25:40).

I began researching Haitian adoptions and discovered they were on hold because of the earthquake. I was also disappointed to learn that John and I didn't qualify to adopt from the country.

God was nudging us toward adoption, but Haiti wasn't an

option. I felt that He was saying, "I have an awesome journey planned for you. Are you going to step out in faith and follow Me? If you do, you're in for the ride of a lifetime."

There was definitely hesitation on both John's and my part, but I believed God had something amazing in store for us. I chose to cast my fears and worries aside, leave the details to God, and follow Him. I didn't want to miss what God had for us.

A week after dinner with our small group, John and I received a phone call that only God could have orchestrated. A couple from our group wanted to know if we were serious about adopting a child. John and I had decided to choose an adoption agency and start the paperwork when we returned from our vacation in February. Although we had no idea how we would pay for an adoption or where we would adopt from, we knew God was asking us to step out in faith and start the process.

"We've been praying about how we can help you and feel like we are supposed to help carry the financial burden of the adoption," our friend said. "You don't have to worry about the money."

Had I heard her correctly? The large price tag of adoption had intimidated John and me. It could have easily been the deal breaker that kept us from pursuing the path God had asked us to take. We had no idea how we would come up with $28,000 to $30,000. We didn't have that kind of money sitting in a bank account. Through tears, I tried to find the words to express how thankful and humbled we were by our friends' generosity.

I handed the phone to John because I couldn't get the words out to tell him the news. Even if I could, I didn't think he would believe me. When our friend shared the news with him, a look of disbelief spread across his face. "Wow, I don't even know what to say," he said. "Thank you so much."

God knew that coming up with the money to pay for the adoption was the hurdle that would have kept John and me from fulfilling His plan. He was already proving He would take care of the details as long as we walked in obedience. That night, I wrote in my journal, "What an amazing testimony of God's power, love, and faithfulness. That He knows every detail and each and every need of His children. *Wow!* I think John and I better hold on tight. We are in for the ride of our lives."

"Whether you turn to the right or to the left, your ears will hear a voice behind you, saying, 'This is the way; walk in it'" (Isaiah 30:21).

Before leaving for vacation, I researched adoption and discovered there would be an information meeting about international adoption the Tuesday after we returned. The meeting was going to be held only a few miles from our house and was the only meeting that particular agency was having in our area for the entire year. God was opening another door.

But there was still one very important question that needed to be answered. From where were we supposed to adopt? We didn't want to choose a country at random, and at that time, we didn't realize that we wouldn't qualify to adopt from every country. We knew God was calling us to adopt, so we were certain He would show us where we were supposed to go. I believed Isaiah 58:11, which says, "The LORD will guide us always." We knew He would guide us to our baby, wherever that might be.

Before the meeting, I prayed for wisdom and discernment. I trusted that God already knew all the details about our child. He sees each of us before we are ever knit together in our mother's womb (Jeremiah 1:3; Psalm 139:13–14). As we sat with other hopeful couples in a small room at the local library, we learned that every country had a long list of requirements that prospective adoptive parents had to meet. We had to be married two years before we could start an international adoption, and even then, we only qualified to adopt from Ethiopia or Russia.

John and I were drawn to Ethiopia for several reasons. First, we could adopt a baby as young as six months old. At the time, it was really important to us that we adopt an infant. I wanted to experience all things baby, even the sleepless nights. Second, in most cases, an extensive medical history is provided for children adopted from Ethiopia. And third, as first-time parents, we couldn't choose the gender of our child, which we preferred for two reasons. First, how would we ever choose between a girl and a boy? Second, we wouldn't get to choose the sex of the baby if we were having a biological child. We both wanted to be surprised. (We later learned that this rule only applied to that particular agency.)

The fourth and final reason we were drawn to Ethiopia was the price tag. The cost of an Ethiopian adoption ranged anywhere from $10,000 to $15,000 less than a Russian adoption. Unfortunately, money did play a factor in our decision, as we did not have an unlimited amount of money in our bank account.

Although these factors definitely influenced our decision, God had answered my prayer for discernment very clearly. When we were told Ethiopia strongly preferred their children to be placed with Christian families, I was sold. I had heard all I needed to hear. God had revealed from where He wanted us to adopt.

John and I were giddy with anticipation as we left the meeting and excited about our future trip to Africa.

⟨∞⟩

If you had asked me prior to January 2010 if I ever thought I would travel across the world to adopt a child, I would have looked at you like you were crazy. Before God placed adoption on my heart, I had never desired to go to a Third World country. I was content living in my safe and comfortable world. But when God placed adoption on my heart, I felt that He continually asked me one question: "Will you step out in faith and follow Me?"

I've studied Hebrews 11 many times. It's often referred to as the Faith Hall of Fame.

Verse eight stands out to me the most: "By faith Abraham, when called to go to a place he would later receive as his inheritance, obeyed and went, even though he did not know where he was going." Next to this verse in my Bible I have written, "Our future adoption, going to Ethiopia. We have to trust God and follow Him, even if we can't see His full plan." Like Abraham, I had to have faith; I had to trust that God would work all the details out perfectly.

When I participated in a Beth Moore study on Hebrews, she encouraged us to add a final verse to the chapter, which was to begin, "By faith, Jennifer ..." I thought about what I would want written beside my name if it appeared in the Faith Hall of Fame. So in my Bible I wrote, "By faith, Jennifer, when called to adopt a child, faithfully followed God as He led her to Ethiopia, trusting that He would provide the finances and take care of all the details because she knew the journey was His plan for her.

She stepped out in faith, not worried about what others thought but in obedience to God."

⎯⎯⎯ ∞∞∞ ⎯⎯⎯

John and I sat opposite my parents at a local Mexican restaurant. I was nervous about telling them our plans to adopt. I feared the worst but hoped for the best.

When the waiter set down our plates of hot, steaming food, I decided I might as well spill it. "As you know, I've been having some medical issues that are keeping us from having a baby." My parents shook their heads; neither of them had reached for their fork. I decided to keep talking and to talk fast. I purged every detail of the past few months and finished with the grand announcement. "We've decided to adopt a baby from Africa."

By the look on my mom's face, it was clear she didn't share in my excitement. My dad sat quietly, unsure of what to say. I chattered nervously, trying to think of anything to make them even the slightest bit excited.

Once my mom got over the initial shock, she rattled off a long list of why adopting a baby from a Third World country wasn't a good idea, including, raising children is hard enough. Were we ready for the challenges of raising a baby of a different race? Finally, she said, "Do what you want. But I wouldn't do it."

"We really believe this is God's plan for us," I said. "I would hate to miss out on something that has the potential to be incredible because of things that are out of my control."

I knew my mom was worried about what people would think. I didn't know of a single family in my hometown that had adopted transracially.

My parents sat in silence, their food untouched. I had a knot in my stomach and felt completely defeated. We sat in awkward silence and picked at our food. I wanted my parents to be excited for us, but it looked like it would take awhile for them to warm up to the news. I was crushed by their reaction, but I knew I had to be obedient to God.

We paid our bill and walked to the car. Not another word was said about our plans.

With our decision to adopt from Ethiopia came the understanding that we would face criticism from people who didn't understand or agree with two white people adopting a brown baby.

There was a brief period of time when I worried about the opinions of others. I didn't care what people thought as much as I worried how I would handle the negative comments, questions, and stares. How would I protect my child from the ugliness? But my fears and concerns began to fade as I dug into God's Word. The following quote by an unknown author completely changed my perspective: "The color of love is always the same in the eyes of a child."

Before adoption, race was not a topic John and I ever discussed. I have never considered myself racist, but I grew up in a predominately white, small Texas town where people didn't intermarry or adopt transracially. I went to high school with less than ten African American students.

But after we decided to adopt from Ethiopia, God began chiseling away my old ways of thinking about race and reminded me to always look deeper than the color of someone's skin. One of my favorite lessons came from Numbers 12.

Moses, a Hebrew, was married to an Ethiopian woman named Zipporah. His sister, Miriam, judged him for marrying Zipporah, likely because of her race. Because Miriam judged Moses, God gave her leprosy. "To regard a race, group or individual as less important than another is sin in view of the fact that Christ died for all people and for each one in particular. At the foot of the cross, we are equal."[1] God does not look at the color of our skin but at our heart.

Our families seemed hesitant about our plan, but there was one person who was thrilled we were going to adopt a baby.

Autry was eight years old and lived in my hometown. My mom began keeping her when she was only a few months old, and she quickly became the center of our attention. Her blond hair, blue eyes, and sassiness stole our hearts. When she found out we were going to adopt from Ethiopia, she could hardly contain her excitement. It was hard explaining to an eight-year-old that it would likely be years before we brought a baby home.

"What do you think the baby will look like?" Autry's mom asked her one day.

"I think it will have blond hair and blue eyes," Autry said.

"I think we better look up some pictures of Ethiopian babies on the computer," her mom said.

Letters from Autry soon began arriving in my mailbox. I looked forward to them during our long wait. Finding a pink or purple envelope waiting for me brightened my day. One day, I smiled when I recognized the familiar handwriting. Autry almost always wrote in pencil. I opened the envelope, unfolded the letter, and my heart began to melt as I read the words.

Dear Jennifer,

I heard you were going to adopt a kid. So we, as in we, I mint Myka, you, and me and the baby could go shopping. So what do you think?

Love, Autry

One the back of the letter, Autry had included a list of possible baby names. There was one column for girl names and another for boy names. At the top of each list she included Autry Jr.

She even sent John a letter.

Dear John,

So how do you feel about adopting a baby? You're going to be a dad. You'll probably be a great dad.

Xoxox,
Autry

We were at dinner, celebrating my sister's graduation from nursing school, when Autry announced, "You're going to travel all the way around the world to bring home your baby!"

"How did you know that?" I asked.

"My mom and I have been doing research on the computer," Autry said. "When you bring your baby home, you'll have to celebrate Gotcha Day."

I couldn't believe how much she had learned about Ethiopia and adoption in general.

"I have a gift for the baby, but I left it at home," Autry said, disappointed.

"That's okay," I said. "You can give it to me the next time I see you."

A few weeks later, we were back in Texas, and Autry stopped by my sister's house to see me. She skipped up the driveway with a gift bag in hand and beamed with delight when she handed it to me.

Tucked between sheets of brightly colored tissue paper was a small, stuffed Pooh Bear. The tissue crinkled as I pulled him out. Pooh was my favorite as a child. "Oh, Autry, I love it," I said as I hugged her.

"It was mine when I was a little girl," Autry said. "My mom washed it in the washing machine. I wanted your baby to have it."

As John and I continued researching adoption agencies, we discovered that an agency in Texas would allow us to submit our application to adopt after only one year of marriage. We were thrilled that we wouldn't have to wait until our second anniversary to start the adoption process. We had met several couples who had used the agency and were confident with the services they provided.

We completed the initial application and arranged to meet with the couple from church who had offered to help pay for the adoption. We just needed to discuss the financial details with them and decided to meet for dinner.

"We have found an agency that will accept our application, and we're ready to start the process," I said.

Our friends congratulated us, but they seemed hesitant. Finally, one of them said, "One of the couples who had planned to help has decided not to. They had agreed because they thought it was a great way to help after the earthquake, but now you aren't adopting from Haiti."

As our friends shared the devastating news, all I could think about was our application sitting on the kitchen table, ready to be mailed the following day. Our dreams of adopting a baby from Ethiopia began slipping away.

I forced myself to smile through the remainder of dinner. It took all I had not to break down and cry. I was heartbroken, defeated, and overwhelmed. I wore a mask of appreciation, but behind it, I was falling apart. I couldn't concentrate on the conversation because I was trying to figure out how John and I would come up with the thousands and thousands of dollars we needed to pay for an adoption.

"We still want to help," our friends said. "We will contribute five thousand dollars toward your adoption." It was a very generous gift, but how in the world would John and I come up with $20,000 to cover the remaining costs?

Once in the car, I crumbled. John tried to be optimistic, but I just wanted to have a pity party. I was hurt and completely overwhelmed by the $20,000 looming over our heads. We had faced one obstacle after another trying to start a family, and I was tired of being optimistic. John left me alone on the front porch while I sobbed uncontrollably.

Later that night, as I lay on the couch talking to God through my tears, I realized the lesson He was trying to teach me. John and I had been relying too much on the financial gift from our friends and not enough on God. God could have provided all the money up front, but that would have been too easy. He wanted to stretch our faith. He wanted to provide the money in ways that we couldn't comprehend and at the exact moment we needed it. A few days, I read the story about Abraham's willingness to sacrifice his only son, Isaac, when God asked him to.

> By faith Abraham, when God tested him, offered Isaac as a sacrifice. He who had received the promises was about to sacrifice his one and only son, even though God had said to him, "It is through Isaac that your offspring will be reckoned." Abraham reasoned that God could raise the dead and figuratively speaking, he did receive Isaac back from death. (Hebrews 11:17–19)

Abraham knew God hadn't fulfilled His plan for Isaac, but he trusted God and was obedient to His call.

"Abraham said to his servants, 'Stay here with the donkey while I and the boy go over there. We will worship and then we will come back to you" (Genesis 22:5), and Abraham told Isaac, "God will himself provide the lamb for the burnt offering my son" And God did. He provided a ram to be used as the sacrifice (Genesis 22:8). Author Kelly Minter wrote,

> Isn't it interesting that Abraham was wrong about the process but right in concept? He was wrong about the details but right about the fact that God would provide. God honored his faith; never giving thought to Abraham's superfluous errors of how it would happen ... Abraham believed God to be a God of provision.[2]

John's and my road was similar to Abraham's. God had called us to adopt from Ethiopia, and although His provision for the adoption hadn't happened like we initially thought it would, we knew He would provide. We believed God was who He said He was: Jehovah-Jireh, "The Lord will provide." (Genesis 22:14)

CHAPTER 3

The Desert

We also rejoice in our suffering because we know
that suffering produces perseverance, perseverance
character, and character hope. And hope does not
disappoint us, because God has poured out his love
into our hearts by the Holy Spirit, whom he has
given us.

—ROMANS 5:3–5

Moses was eighty years old when he wandered the
desert. He was minding his own business, tending
his flock, when all of a sudden the angel of the Lord
appeared to him amidst the flames of a burning bush. Moses
noticed that although the bush continued to burn, it wasn't
burning up. He thought it was interesting, so he decided to
investigate. When he got closer, Moses received the surprise of
his life.

"Moses! Moses!" God called.

"Here I am," Moses replied.

God told Moses that He had seen the misery of His people in
Egypt. He had heard their cries and was concerned about their
suffering (I don't know about you, but that comforts me.) Then

God revealed His plan: Moses would lead the Israelites out of Egypt (read Exodus 3).

Just as God had walked beside Moses in the desert, He walked beside me in mine. God's plans are often revealed during the desert seasons of our lives. His plans will often change the course of our lives if we choose to walk in obedience.

It didn't take long for John and me to realize that God's plan to build our family through adoption would change us. Actually, it more or less rocked our world. God plucked us out of our selfish comfort zone and gave us eyes to see a world beyond ourselves in desperate need of Jesus. But the revelation didn't come without pain and suffering.

I was like a balloon on the verge of bursting, filled with excitement about our future adoption but also grieving my inability to have children. Our families weren't completely on board with our idea to adopt—especially a brown child from a Third World country. People questioned why we had given up on having our own children. "Why aren't you giving fertility treatments a try?" they would ask. "You know, people who adopt almost always end up pregnant." Add to that the fact that we still needed about $20,000 to pay for our adoption. I felt utterly hopeless. Becoming a mother seemed so far out of reach.

As I tried to make sense of my raging emotions, my best friend from high school welcomed her second child. As I stared at photos of Amber cradling her sweet baby girl, my heart ached. It seemed like just yesterday that she had held her firstborn for the first time, and I vividly remembered the emotions that overcame me as I looked at photos of her holding her tiny bundle of joy wrapped in blue.

The day Amber gave birth to her first child was when my baby fever kicked into high gear. Watching Amber become a mommy made me desperately want to be a mommy too. As I looked through the photos of her family and friends waiting in eager anticipation for the arrival of her second child, a thought flashed through my mind: I would never experience family and friends gathered in a hospital waiting room awaiting the birth of my baby. Not experiencing the epidural or the labor pains was one thing, but likely never experiencing the hospital waiting room moment was another and made me very sad.

Then God reminded me that there would be people waiting for the arrival of my child. It wouldn't be in a hospital waiting room but in baggage claim at the airport. When we stepped off that plane from Ethiopia, our loved ones would be there to greet us.

There were certain things associated with pregnancy that I was sad to miss. I would never see a plus sign on a pregnancy test or surprise John with the news that he was going to be a dad. I would never feel a baby kick from inside of me. But I would experience things other mothers never would. An unexpected phone call saying that John and I had a referral, and sitting down at the computer, opening an e-mail, and seeing the face of our child for the first time. We would surprise our family and reveal the gender of our child and show off his or her pictures. And just like any first-time parents, we would decorate a nursery and register at Target and Babies R Us. We would travel across the world to bring our baby home, and at the end of it all, I wouldn't have to lose baby weight or worry about stretch marks.

There's a myth in the adoption world that once you start the adoption process you are guaranteed to get pregnant. I don't know how many times people reminded me of the myth. "Now that you're adopting, you know what's going to end up happening," they would say. "You'll get pregnant." Yes, it does happen. We knew couples who became pregnant either in the midst of their adoption or shortly after adopting a child.

Certain people in my life constantly brought up the topic of pregnancy and questioned why I didn't want biological children. With each comment, I felt like someone was stabbing me in the back and twisting the knife as hard as they could. They may not have said the words, but with each comment, I heard, "Adoption isn't as good as having a biological child." Becoming a mother through adoption was hard enough without people wishing I would have a baby the old-fashioned way. It was hard for several people in my life to accept that I might never (and really didn't want) to have biological children.

One friend constantly asked if I was pregnant. When I told her we were planning to adopt, she responded, "You know that adoption is a big responsibility." Like having biological children isn't?

Others pushed and pushed for us to give fertility treatments a try. "Have you just given up on having your own children?" a family member asked.

"Our child from Ethiopia *will* be my child." I said as calmly as I could.

I spent months grieving, praying, and dealing with my infertility. God had made it clear that I would become a mother through adoption, and I was at peace with that plan. I just wished others couple accept it too.

Getting pregnant at that point in our adoption process in all honesty would have been devastating. Our adoption would have been put on hold, and we were already facing an extremely long wait.

I wrote the following blog post addressing the myth that everyone who adopts ends up pregnant:

> I understand that not everyone agrees with adoption, that not everyone grasps a woman who is okay with never experiencing pregnancy. You don't have to agree with my choice or understand God's path for me. But please consider how hurtful your comments are when you act like you're anything but excited about our adoption because in your eyes it's not the "right" way to become a mother.

Cheerful Christmas music blared from my radio. "It's the hap, happiest time of the year" filled the air as tears gushed from my eyes. It was one of those ugly cries, the kind where you can't stop the tears no matter how hard you try. And of course, I had no Kleenex. I wiped my tears (and my nose) with one of my gloves. I love Christmas, and I especially love Christmas music. I start playing it before Thanksgiving, which drives John crazy. But that year, it was not the "hap, happiest" time for me.

Most mornings, I prayed during my drive to work. But that morning, I couldn't find the words or the strength to pray. I just cried. I took comfort in knowing that God knew my heart. Romans 8:26 came to mind: "In the same way, the Spirit helps us in our weakness. We do not know what we ought to pray for, but the Spirit himself intercedes for us with groans that words cannot express." The previous day, a friend had reminded me that I could be confident that God had heard the cries of my heart even when it seemed like there was nothing but silence.

To say that I had been struggling at that point in our adoption journey would have been an understatement. I was grieving my inability to have a biological child. The massive stack of adoption paperwork piled on our kitchen table overwhelmed me, and I was aggravated with my husband for not being as eager to complete the paperwork as I was. In fact, completing the paperwork consumed me. So many things were out of my control, but turning the paperwork into our agency as quickly as possible was something I could control. The sooner we turned in the paperwork, the sooner the gaping hole in my heart would be filled.

The desert was lonely. The majority of my friends and family were unaware of the emotional roller coaster I was on. I yearned to reach out to them, to let them into the dry places that zapped every ounce of energy and joy I had. I desperately wanted to spill my guts, to find someone who could understand what I was going through, yet I couldn't find the words to explain the turmoil I truly felt inside.

One morning, I picked up the phone to call my dad. I wanted him to tell me it would be okay, but I put the phone down before I pushed his number on speed dial. How could I reach out to him when my parents weren't completely on board with our decision to adopt in the first place? The few times I had broached my infertility with my mom, her advice had been to relax and let nature take its course. She didn't get that nature *couldn't* take its course.

I was frustrated with myself for feeling depressed. My faith was strong, and from the depths of my soul, I believed that God had a perfect plan. He would work everything out for His good. So why couldn't I snap out of my gloomy mood?

I spent many days crying in my car during lunch, the majority of the time unable to pinpoint why I was crying in the first place. The sad days outweighed the happy ones.

Then one night, I was up late, flipping through TV channels, when I stumbled across a Christian network interviewing the lead singer of the band FFH. Jeromy was diagnosed with MS in 2007 and was talking about suffering. What he said something resonated in my spirit. "Suffering doesn't have to be physical pain. It can be losing a job, waiting on something. It can be a desert season."

I was suffering.

"Suffering is not just for some people, and it's not optional," he said. "But there is joy because suffering is where Jesus meets us in special ways."

For months, I had been suffering emotionally. I had been waiting on something my heart desired and longed for, unsure of when that desire would be met. In the midst of suffering, my only option was to cling to Jesus.

Christians often think they are excluded from suffering. Once we surrender our lives to Christ, we think the road should be smooth, without potholes and detours, but the Word is clear:

"We also rejoice in our sufferings because we know that suffering produces perseverance, perseverance character, and character hope" (Romans 5:3). And Romans 8:18 says, "We should consider our present sufferings not worth comparing to the glory that will be revealed in us."

That night, FFH performed a song that described my life perfectly in that moment.

> And this may not be the road I would choose for me
> but it still feels right somehow.
> And I have never felt you as close to me
> as I do right now.
> So this is what it feels like to be led.[1]

My initial plan to have a family did not include adoption, but God had chosen the path for me. Through my suffering and the long road to motherhood, I drew closer to God and felt His presence more than I ever had before. He was leading me. There was a purpose for my pain.

———— ∞∞∞ ————

Mother's Day was much harder than I had anticipated. John tried making it special by delivering a Classic 50's Dr. Pepper and a Mother's Day card to me in bed, but the emptiness in my heart, the longing for a child, was still there.

At church, several people wished me Happy Mother's Day, which brought joy to my grieving heart. For them to acknowledge me on Mother's Day was the sweetest gift I could have received since in my mind I was already a mother. I just hadn't seen the face of my child yet. A baby wasn't growing in my womb, but my heart was about to burst with love for my future son or daughter. That Mother's Day was filled with hope and longing for the day I would no longer have empty arms, but it was also a day of heartache.

During the baby dedication at church that day, our pastor shared the verse I chose to paint on our nursery wall.

"I prayed for this child and the Lord granted what I asked of him," my pastor read. As he read 1 Samuel 1:27, words that had brought so much hope over the past year, I was overcome with gut-wrenching emotion.

I had spent so much time praying for my children. First, it was that God would allow me to get pregnant. Then in tears and on my knees before the Lord, I released that dream and prayed for God's will to be done. Since that day, He made His plan for my family very clear. I would travel across the world to bring home my children. He had replaced my need to get pregnant with a love for adoption, the orphaned, and Africa. I thanked God for my children that Mother's Day because He was already preparing the way to unite our family.

After the baby dedication, a video was shown where kids answered questions about their moms. "Why do you love your mom?" "How are you and your mom alike?" "How are you and your mom different?" The answer to the last question from a small child pierced my heart. "I am brown, and my mom is tan." A drawing of a dark brown baby and a white mommy appeared on the screen.

The floodgates opened. That was going to be me. That was the family portrait God was painting, and I couldn't wait to see the completed masterpiece. As I sat in church, tears streaming down my face, I wanted to freeze time. I never wanted to forget the heartache of not having a child. I prayed that when I was changed my hundredth dirty diaper and wiped another snotty nose that I would remember how desperately I had wanted the title of mommy.

Adoption isn't always celebrated with as much enthusiasm as a nine-month pregnancy. I wanted to remember my Mother's Day as a waiting mama. I wanted to always acknowledge waiting mothers and the pain that comes from empty arms and longing hearts because so often they are forgotten.

I lost count of the number of times I couldn't find the words or the strength to pray, but God was always faithful, and His presence was overwhelming. One morning, He reminded me that my suffering had an eternal purpose. I had been so consumed by my grief that I had neglected to see the desert from God's perspective.

When I turned my gaze away from myself and toward Jesus, I realized that God wanted to use the dry, parched places of my life to minister to others. So many people were wandering in the desert, desperate for a Savior.

John and I knew several people who needed to experience the amazing love of their heavenly Father. God reminded me that, through our story, John and I could point those individuals to Him. Overcome by emotion, I prayed, "God, if being in the desert means that one person will come to know You as his or her personal savior, I don't want to be anywhere else. I will stay right where I'm at if it means people will see Your amazing power through this difficult season I'm facing. I want You to be glorified."

Kelly Minter once wrote,

> It's all been about faith. Because we trusted Him, He gave us the grace to walk through it even when we thought we weren't going to make it. Not only did He reveal His miracles firsthand to increase our faith, but the people surrounding us also got to see that each blessing was coming from God alone.[2]

I had a new outlook on the desert. There *was* a purpose that went far beyond myself.

Habakkuk 1:5 says, "Look among the nations! Observe! Be astonished! Wonder! Because I am doing something in your days you would not believe even if you were told." I prayed others would see God's hand in every detail of our adoption and that through our obedience God would do the miraculous in their lives.

———— ⊗ ————

"Now I want you to know, brothers, that what has happened to me has really served to advance the gospel" (Philippians 1:12). I rolled this verse around in my head and underlined it in my Bible. Next to it, in blue ink I wrote, "My infertility, our adoption, a powerful testimony of God's power. Let it advance the gospel."

Paul faced prison, a trial, and many painful and desperate situations. Yet in the midst of so much suffering and hardship, he remained thankful, joyful, and content. He focused on Jesus instead of his circumstances and knew every trial was being used for God's glory.

I wanted to be like Paul. I was determined to focus on Jesus during the grueling wait instead of focusing on my empty arms and heart. I wanted to become more like my Father as I waited. I prayed that in the midst of the hard stuff, when my heart ached for children, I would have hopeful contentment like Paul.

I continued uttering the prayer that had completely changed the way I viewed the desert season I found myself in. "Lord, let others see you through our journey. May every step be for your glory." I told God over and over that if the stuff I was going through helped only one person see His glory, power, and grace, it was worth staying in the hot, dry place. So many times, through tears, I surrendered to Him until it became a daily occurrence. I knew the pain and heartache would be worth it if someone's life was transformed by the love of Jesus.

CHAPTER 4

One Dollar at a Time

But as for me, I will always have hope; I will praise
you more and more.

—PSALM 71:14

Eventually, John and I recovered from the sting of learning
we no longer had the adoption money. We were ready to
do whatever it took to bring our baby home and began
brainstorming every possible way to come up with the funds.
John insisted he would take a cargo plane to Ethiopia if he had
to. We had already fallen in love with an Ethiopian child that we
had yet to lay eyes on. We were determined to raise the money
some way, somehow.

As I poured over adoption blogs, I quickly noticed a
common theme—adoption fund-raising. The majority of
families pursuing international adoption had to do some sort
of fund-raising.

We decided to send a letter to our family and friends,
explaining our desire to adopt and the steep price tag associated
with international adoption and humbly asking for their support
as we worked toward bringing our child home.

Dear Family, Friends, and Colleagues,

We are writing you today with a special request on our hearts. We are about to begin the life-changing journey of adoption, and we need your support as we begin working toward bringing home our "Missing Linck" from Ethiopia.

The adoption costs are quite high. We need to raise approximately $18,000, and we are humbly asking if you would prayerfully consider helping us bring our baby home.

This adoption journey is about so much more than becoming parents. For us, it's about fulfilling the amazing plan of a loving, powerful, and faithful God. We want to step out in faith and open our hearts and our home to a child in need of a family, love, security, and hope for the future.

Adopting a baby from Ethiopia means that his or her life may literally be saved. There are millions of AIDS orphans in Ethiopia, and one million children are killed by malaria each year. At the very least, our child will have opportunities for education, nutrition, medical care, and, most of all, spiritual growth that he or she might not be afforded in his or her native country.

Our goal is to save and raise money during the next three months so we can submit our adoption application on our two-year wedding anniversary in October. In order for that to happen, we need to raise $18,000 to cover the initial adoption fees and the two trips to Ethiopia that we are required to take during the adoption process.

We can't fathom the emotions that we will experience when we lay eyes on our child for the first time. Because, you see, we are already in love with this child, and we don't even know him or her. But we have peace in knowing that our God does! He knew every detail about our baby long before he or she was created in his or her mother's womb (Jeremiah 1:5).

If you can help us financially or support us through prayer, we would be so grateful. To make a donation, you can mail a check, and we will deposit it into an adoption savings account that has been set up for our fund-raising efforts. You can also donate toward our adoption using PayPal on our adoption website.

If we can answer any questions, please feel free to call or e-mail us. We would love to share our reasons for adopting. You can follow our journey and get the latest updates on our adoption website.

Thank you for your love and support!
John and Jennifer Linck

We mailed the letter and prayed that God would stir hearts to want to help us.

We were very surprised by the people who chose to support us. It definitely wasn't the people we had expected. We faced criticism from family and friends who didn't support our decision to fund-raise.

As I continued reading adoption blogs and talked to other adopting families, I realized John and I weren't crazy to ask for help. Most families don't have an extra twenty grand sitting in their bank account. I was just going to have to get thicker skin if I was going to survive our journey.

But people were hateful. "You don't ask others to pay so you can have a biological child," someone said. *(Of course not. That's what health insurance is for.)* "We just don't understand how you can be asking for money for something like this," others said. John and I didn't expect family and friends to hand over big, fat checks; we just wanted their support.

As I talked to God about my hurt feelings and the criticism, He quickly spoke to my heart. Once again, He didn't want John and me to depend on other people. He wanted us to cling to Him. His still, small voice reminded me of something I should have already learned: "People will let you down. I will not."

John and I met with our financial adviser who told us we could borrow against our retirement account if it was the only way to pay for the adoption. John and I were willing to do that, but we believed we could raise the majority of the money through saving and fund-raising.

The response from our letter wasn't what we had hoped for, so it was time to put our fund-raising ideas to the test. I love to bake and had purchased a cookie cutter in the shape of Africa (proceeds from the purchase of the cookie cutter went to help another family in the process of adopting from Ethiopia). I decided to make and sell Africa-shaped sugar cookies as our first official fund-raiser.

Within days of announcing the cookie sales, twenty-five dozen cookies had already been ordered. After a month of being up to my eyeballs in cookie dough, we had sold seventy-five dozen cookies and raised almost $1,000. I literally wore out the first cookie cutter I bought. The edges became dull, and I had to order another one to keep up with the cookie demands.

When the last cookie was baked, iced, boxed up, and delivered, I never wanted to see another cookie again. But I loved seeing God work through our hard work and fund-raising efforts.

Some days we received several donations in the mail, and other days we would sell a single "Bringing Home the Missing Linck" t-shirt. But every day, even in the smallest way, God reminded me that He would provide the money we needed for the adoption.

God continually surprised us with the ways He chose to provide. Donations came from people we barely knew and blog readers I had never met. John came home from work one day and handed me an envelope. Tucked inside was a check for $2,000. People's generosity made our chins fall to the ground more than once.

I learned an amazing lesson about sacrifice from my friend's thirteen-year-old daughter as we prepared for a garage sale to continue working toward our goal of $18,000.

My friend called me after she dropped off donations for the garage sale. "Inside one of the boxes is a small plastic bag with money in it," she said. "Morgan wanted to donate the money she has been saving to your adoption fund."

I choked back tears, thinking of Morgan's sacrifice for a child she didn't know. I found the plastic bag and pulled out the most precious and meaningful fifteen dollars I had ever received. The donation meant more than any other gift we received because of the heart of the giver.

Morgan had given everything she had without wanting anything in return.

I was reminded of the widow's offering in Luke 21. The rich were putting extravagant gifts into the temple treasury. Jesus, however, wasn't moved by them. What caught His eye was the widow who placed two small copper coins into the treasury as an offering. Jesus said, "This poor widow has put in more than all the others. All these people gave their gifts out of their wealth; but she out of her poverty put in all she had to live on" (Luke 21:3-4).

After Morgan offered such a beautiful sacrifice on our behalf, I felt the Lord asking me what I was willing to sacrifice to meet the financial needs of our adoption. With each Bible study I completed, each sermon I heard or book I read, a common theme surfaced: sacrifice. God didn't want me finding my security in the things of the world. He wanted me to be willing to step out of my comfort zone. How could I be more like Morgan? Would I give everything I had for the sake of my child?

For weeks, God continued bringing the same thing to my mind. Was I willing to sell my wedding ring? I was embarrassed to admit that it was worth the amount we lacked to pay the initial adoption fees. There was a time in my life when I was determined to have a big rock on my finger, and I didn't care what it cost John.

But through the adoption process, God changed my heart. He began by pruning the materialistic places in my heart. Eventually, the things of the world began to seem less important. I felt guilty wearing something of such value when that money would have covered our adoption fees. I couldn't imagine choosing my ring over the child waiting across the world for me.

I struggled with guilt over the value of the ring, but I still battled with my flesh over whether or not to sell it. After all, it *was* my wedding ring. And John had the ring made especially for me. Seven small diamonds sat on either side of the center stone, symbolic of our first date. He had gotten down on one knee on a gorgeous beach in Maui shortly after the sun peeked over the horizon and slipped the sparkly diamond on my finger.

David Platt, in his book *Radical*, stated, "Sacrifice is giving away what it hurts to give," but we must remember that "God is committed to providing abundant resources to support those who are living according to His purpose."[1] I was willing to sell my ring for an eternal purpose in hope that others would witness God's glory through our adoption. What if our story led someone to Christ? What if it was only because of adoption that a child in Ethiopia heard about Jesus?

As Platt said,

> I had a choice. I could cling to short-term treasures that I couldn't keep, or I could live for long-term treasures that I couldn't lose: people coming to Christ; men, women, and children living because they now have food; unreached tribes receiving the gospel; and the all-consuming satisfaction of knowing and experiencing Christ as the treasure above all else.[2]

We took my ring to several jewelry stores, eager to see how much we could get for it, but each time we left disappointed. Not a single jeweler was willing to pay even half of its appraised amount. At one store, we were told the ring would be melted down because they were only interested in the diamonds. A friend had tried selling an expensive engagement ring online with no luck.

I confided my frustration to a friend. Why would God ask me to sacrifice my ring when nobody was willing to pay what it was appraised for or anything close to what it was worth? "Maybe the Lord is testing you the way He tested Abraham when he asked him to sacrifice Isaac," she said. "Maybe it is a test to strengthen your faith, to make sure you are really putting your trust in God, but that He doesn't plan for you to really give up your wedding ring."

I thought about what she said as I read the story in Genesis 22. Prior to God testing Abraham, He had given him a promise concerning his son Isaac. "Lift the boy up and take him by the hand, for I will make him into a great nation," the Lord said. (Genesis 21:18). Then the unthinkable happened. God asked Abraham to sacrifice his only son. And Abraham obeyed.

> When they reached the place God had told him about, Abraham built an altar there and arranged the wood on it. He bound his son Isaac and laid him on the altar, on top of the wood. Then he reached out his hand and took the knife to slay his son. But the angel of the LORD called out to him from heaven, "Abraham! Abraham!" "Here I am," he replied. "Do not lay a hand on the boy," he said. "Do not do anything to him. Now I know that you fear God, because you have not

withheld from me your son, your only son."
(Genesis 22:9–12)

The Lord provided a ram as the sacrifice for the burnt offering, and Abraham called that place, "The Lord Will Provide." And the Lord blessed Abraham for his faith and obedience. "And without faith it is impossible to please God because anyone who comes to him must believe He exists and that He rewards those who earnestly seek him" (Hebrews 11:6).

Sometimes God chooses to stretch our faith by asking us to surrender something of great value. In Abraham's case, it was his only son. In my case, it was my wedding ring. Despite what God asks us to sacrifice, to pass the test, we must step out in faith, release our tight grip, and stand before the Lord with open hands.

Fund-raising was hard work. Our critics assumed we were begging for a handout, but that was far from the truth. John and I brainstormed every possible way to save money. We were up to our elbows in cookie dough. The palms of my hands were sore from smashing cookie dough thin enough to cut the perfect Africa shape. We packaged and mailed t-shirts right and left and organized a golf tournament in just two short months. We prayed every day that those donating would see God's hand in our journey. Fund-raising gave us a chance to share our story, which meant people were hearing about Jesus and His incredible love for the orphan, the lost, and the broken.

Fund-raising became more than a means to pay for our adoption. God used fund-raising to open my spiritual eyes to something I'd been blind to or maybe just refused to see. As a Christian, I'm called to help the poor, the orphan, and the widow.

It's not a choice. God's Word is very clear. "Pure and genuine religion in the sight of God the Father means caring for orphans and widows in their distress and refusing to let the world corrupt you" (James 1:27). Not everyone is called to adopt, but every Christian can do something to support adoption. Supporting families who have chosen to adopt is one way we can live out the call Christ has placed on our lives in James 1:27. We can literally be the hands and feet of Jesus when we bear the financial burden adoptive families face.

Adoptive families extended their hands to help us and other adoptive families countless times. We, too, gave to others, offering what we could to help bring orphans to their Forever Families.

Witnessing the camaraderie among the adoption community was a joy, even though each family was trying to raise a large amount of money to bring their children home. It was a beautiful picture of what God calls his children to do. "Give and it will be given to you. A good measure, pressed down, shaken together and running over, will be poured into your lap. For with the measure you use, it will be measured to you" (Luke 6:38).

<hr />

We organized a dinner and silent auction with two other couples also in the process of adopting from Ethiopia. We hoped the benefit would not only bring in funds but would also raise awareness about adoption and orphan care among our family and friends. We all agreed that we would deem the event a success if each couple walked away with $500 in their pocket.

We spent several months arranging affordable catering, asking local businesses for donations, advertising our event, and creating fun gift baskets to auction off. We were thrilled by the response from local business owners and received amazing donations, including autographed Oklahoma City Thunder memorabilia.

Both John's family and my family came to Oklahoma for the event, and for the first time, it felt like we were all working toward the same goal—bringing our child home. Before the event, we stood together and prayed, asking the Lord to use the auction for His glory and told Him we trusted Him with the rest.

The night exceeded our expectations. More than one hundred people attended. Our moms worked hard all night in the kitchen serving large helpings of pasta, and our dads helped with the silent auction and purchased their fair share of raffle tickets. During the dinner, we showed a video that followed one couple's journey to Ethiopia to meet their child. When the caretaker placed the brown-skinned baby into the arms of his American mother, my breath caught in my throat.

I glanced over and saw my parents and sister wiping tears from their eyes. In that moment, I knew they were finally beginning to understand the crazy dream God had placed on our hearts.

Our families caught a glimpse of the eternal purpose God had for our journey. Surrounded by other families who had adopted children from Africa, they saw that families made up of white parents and brown babies weren't uncommon. We were not going to be the first biracial family, and we wouldn't be the last.

When the last auction item was paid for and the final guest left, we counted what we had raised. Each couple and their families gathered for the big announcement. You could feel the anticipation.

"Drum roll, please," said our friend's sister. "The grand total from tonight's event is $4,918.50."

Applause and cheers rang out. Wiping away tears, we stood shocked at what God had provided.

We had only asked for $500 per couple, but God had given out of His abundance.

Once again, God proved Himself faithful. Our families got to witness firsthand that when God calls His children to something that seems crazy and impossible, He always provides the means to accomplish the task.

Natalie Grant sings,

> I'll make a way;
> I'll do whatever it takes,
> even though it won't be easy.
> I have a plan and though you may not understand,
> today I'll make a way.[3]

Those words touch a deep place in my soul each time I hear them. In July 2010, I was heartbroken and overwhelmed when we learned that the majority of the funds we needed for our adoption were no longer available. I sat on my front porch, defeated and sobbing hysterically, uncertain of how we would ever come up with $25,000. Seven months later, I was in complete awe of how God provided the money we needed. We had raised $18,000.

After selling seventy-five dozen Africa-shaped cookies, organizing a golf tournament, having a garage sale, selling cookie jars for Christmas and cupcakes for Valentine's Day, and through many, many generous donations, we had reached our goal. God cared so much about the future of my child and provided every penny John and I needed for the initial fees. I had no doubt He would provide the rest. We were more than halfway there.

CHAPTER 5

Chasing Paper Just to Wait

> But I've raised you up for this very purpose, that I
> might show you my power and that my name might
> be proclaimed in all the earth.
>
> —EXODUS 9:16

Adoption is comprised of paperwork and waiting. Agency applications and government-required paperwork littered my kitchen table the first six months of our process. About the time I thought I had answered the last question, someone else needed something in writing to prove we were capable of raising a child.

Completing the paperwork became a full-time job. The majority of my time was spent standing in long lines at the post office to mail documents or at the bank getting paperwork notarized.

We were on a scavenger hunt for birth certificates, marriage license, copies of driver's licenses, statements from our employers, letters from our bank, and medical clearances. And that was just the first round of documents. Every t had to be crossed and every i dotted. The slightest mistake would result in a major setback in our adoption. Something as simple as completing paperwork became a nightmare.

John and I needed a letter from our bank stating that we were in good standing. The agency had very specific guidelines for what the letter could and couldn't say, but the bank manager was making it impossible to get what we needed.

"I'm sorry, sir," the manager said. "I can't issue a letter. It's against our policy."

"What do you mean you can't give me a letter?" John asked, trying to keep his cool. "You don't seem to understand. We have to have a letter from you or we can't proceed with our adoption."

"I'm sorry, sir. I can't help you."

I sank into a nearby chair and began to cry. Why was this so complicated? My frustration grew as the manager continued to deny our request, not the slightest bit concerned about the significance of the letter. "Sir, I understand you're frustrated, but there's really nothing I can do."

John snapped. "Don't tell me you understand. When you have spent months collecting documents to prove to some agency that you're capable of being a parent, *then* you can say you understand."

We left the bank defeated and empty-handed.

A few hours later, John's cell phone rang. The bank manager had drafted the letter we had requested, and we could pick it up at our convenience. I guess he felt sorry for the crazy people having an emotional breakdown in his lobby.

It was my twenty-ninth birthday. To celebrate, I enjoyed a wonderful lunch with my coworkers. As we drove back to the office, I decided to check my e-mail on my phone. Excitement bubbled up within me when I noticed the unread message from our agency in my inbox. I opened it and began to read. "As of February 23, 2011, you are considered agency approved and can proceed with your Ethiopian adoption," the e-mail stated. Four months after starting the paper chase, I received the best birthday gift I could have hoped for! My coworkers cheered as I cried happy tears, and we celebrated the milestone in our adoption journey.

Now John and I would wait to receive appointments to be fingerprinted at the local Homeland Security office, which would then be submitted to Washington, DC. Then we would wait for our I600-A approval. The Application for Advance Processing of Orphan Petition had to be filed with the US Citizenship and Immigration Services before John and I could be approved to adopt from Ethiopia.

Each step was bringing us closer to Ethiopia.

As we waited for our I600-A approval, we began hearing devastating news about the future of Ethiopian adoptions. The Ethiopian government planned to cut adoptions by 90 percent, and the adoption community was in a frenzy. Many families were just weeks away from being placed on the wait list, and the cutbacks threatened to increase their wait time dramatically.

John and I knew when we chose international adoption that there would be a lot of waiting involved and that things weren't likely to go as originally planned. International adoption is unpredictable.

After learning about the possible decrease in Ethiopian adoptions, we scheduled a conference call with our agency. We discussed what we could expect once we were considered a waiting family. With all the uncertainty in Ethiopia, John and I definitely had questions and concerns.

Our caseworker informed us that once we were placed on the official wait list, it would be at least twelve months before we received a referral.

We lacked several steps before we could be put on the wait list. We had to be fingerprinted, receive our approval letter, and our dossier (which was ready and waiting) had to be sent to Washington to be translated before it could be sent to Ethiopia. We prayed we would be on the wait list by late April or early May 2011. If that happened, we would likely receive a referral summer 2012.

We had initially thought we would be traveling to Ethiopia during the summer of 2012.

Habakkuk 2:3 comforted me during those initial days of uncertainty. "If it seems slow in coming, wait patiently, for it will surely take place. It will not be delayed." God's timing was perfect. I was desperate to get on a plane and travel to my baby, but I had to be patient. I trusted that the Lord was working out the details and believed that at the end of the crazy journey, there would be a baby girl or baby boy who would be worth the wait. I had to trust that God's plan was better than my own. "For my thoughts aren't your thoughts, neither are your ways my ways, declares the LORD. As the heavens are higher than the earth, so are my ways higher than your ways and my thoughts than your thoughts" (Isaiah 55:8–9).

The rumor was that the Ethiopian government would hear approximately twenty adoption cases per day, thirty less than normal. The news wasn't great, but it was a glimmer of hope to families waiting to be united with their children. At one point,

Ethiopian officials had considered cutting adoption cases to five per day.

As I prayed about the situation, I began sensing that the negative changes were just a way for "God to show his power and for His name to be proclaimed in all the earth" (Exodus 9:16). The situation was completely out of my control. The only thing I could do was pray. I had to believe God would hold true to His promise to care for the millions of innocent orphans who were in desperate need of families.

Matthew 7:7–8 says, "Ask and it will be given to you; seek and you will find; knock and the door will be opened to you. For everyone who asks receives, he who seeks finds; and to him who knocks, the door will be opened." Many people prayed around the clock for Peter when he was imprisoned, and because of their faithful prayers, he was released. Upon his release, the angel of the Lord brought Peter to the door where the group was praying. But when the group saw Peter, they didn't believe it was him.

They prayed but didn't believe. They asked but didn't expect God to answer. Was I praying and actually believing that God could move the mountains standing in the way of Ethiopian adoptions? Was I expecting Him to move on behalf of the five million orphans in Ethiopia?

Isaiah 42:16 says, "I will lead the blind by ways they have not known, along unfamiliar paths I will guide them; I will turn darkness into light before them and make the rough places smooth. These are the things I will do, I will not forsake them." God was bigger than the Ethiopian government, and He could move the mountains on behalf of the families in limbo. When we are afraid and uncertain of what we are up against, we can rest, knowing that God has things under control. "When you pass through the waters, I will be with you; and when you pass through the rivers, they will not sweep over you. When you walk through the fire, you will not be burned; the flames will not set you ablaze" (Isaiah 43:2).

———— ❧ ————

I was thrilled that we were about to take the final step we needed to complete our dossier. As we walked into the local Department of Homeland Security to have our biometric fingerprints taken, our adoption suddenly felt very real. Once we received approval from Homeland Security, our dossier would be on its way to Ethiopia, and we would officially be considered a waiting family.

As I sat in the waiting area, I thanked God for His sovereignty. Earlier that day, our agency had sent an e-mail informing us that the Ethiopian government would process forty adoption cases a day. John and I were ecstatic.

An Asian lady sitting next to me stared at me curiously. "Why are you here?" she finally asked.

"We are adopting a baby from Africa, so we have to be fingerprinted," I explained.

A huge smile spread across her face. "From Africa?" she asked. "That's a long ways away."

"It is," I said.

"Congratulations," she said. She then asked a few more questions about our adoption as we waited our turn. I was so excited about our adoption that I could have talked to the stranger all day.

———— ❧ ————

In early April 2011, I received an e-mail from my friend Kathleen. She and her husband were a few weeks ahead of us in the adoption process. We had stumbled upon each other's blogs in the early stages of our adoptions, discovered we lived less than thirty miles from one another, and a friendship quickly developed.

Kathleen's e-mail said the State Department had released a statement saying significant delays remained likely for cases presented to Ethiopia's Ministry of Women, Children, and Youth Affairs. It read, "Prospective adoptive parents who did not reach the court summons stage before March 8, 2011, should expect significant delays in the progression of their paperwork through the Government of Ethiopia."

Blog posts by other families in the Ethiopia program confirmed the news. Many were saying that it could take a year to receive a court date after getting a referral. When John and I started our adoption, we had hoped to complete the entire process within eighteen months.

That night I cracked. For the first time since hearing the disturbing news from Ethiopia, I felt hopeless. My stomach churned at the thought of the long wait that loomed ahead of us. It seemed like we were *never* going to get on that plane to bring our child home. I had fallen madly in love with a country whose soil my feet had never touched. I was starting to doubt if they ever would.

Joseph was seventeen when God revealed through two separate dreams that he would rule over his family. But it was years before Joseph saw God's plan fulfilled. He was sold into slavery by his jealous brothers, taken to Egypt where he lived as a trusted slave to Potiphar, and thrown into prison on false accusations. In the midst of so many setbacks, Joseph never lost hope in God.

The Bible says, "The LORD was with Joseph" (Genesis 39:2) at every point of his journey.

God used Joseph's arrogance, his brother's jealousy, and the prison sentence to fulfill the plan He had revealed to Joseph so many years before. Joseph would ultimately save his family from death and famine.

> And now, do not be distressed and do not be angry with yourselves for selling me here, because it was to save lives that God sent me ahead of you. For two years now there has been famine in the land, and for the next five years there will not be plowing and reaping. But God sent me ahead of you to preserve for you a remnant on earth and to save your lives by a great deliverance. So then, it was not you who sent me here, but God. (Genesis 45:5–8)

I had no idea how long I would have to wait before my dream of motherhood became a reality. One year? Two? I wasn't the first (or the last) person facing a longer-than-anticipated wait when it came to the dreams God had placed on my heart. I had to trust in the promise of Psalm 57: "I call to God Most High, to God who fulfills His purpose for me. My heart is confident, God, my heart is confident. I will sing; I will sing praises." (Psalms 57:2,7)

I was in a funk and needed to focus on something other than the grim news coming from Ethiopia. So I decided to start working on the nursery. I had an urge to nest and get things ready for our baby even though it looked like it would be years before a nursery was needed. Pregnant women are constantly reminded that a little one is on the way—morning sickness, a growing belly, swollen feet, and ultrasounds. I needed something to keep me busy and to remind me that a child would be sleeping in the crib someday.

I wanted to clear out the office and set up the crib. I wanted to prepare my home and my heart for what we were anticipating. I wanted to sit in the rocking chair and pray for our children. I wanted to daydream about what it would be like to rock my babies to sleep, feed them, and read to them.

Unfortunately, John didn't understand the whole nesting idea. He wasn't as eager to pack up his stein collection and transform his little corner of our home into a baby haven. His hesitation irritated the fire out of me.

I sat in the middle of the soon-to-be nursery and bawled, overwhelmed by all the junk we had collected over the years. Stuff we would have to get rid of or store in the attic.

"We have plenty of time to figure out what to do with everything," John said, trying to reassure me. He would have been satisfied to stash the junk somewhere the week before we boarded a plane or, better yet, to decorate the nursery with beer steins. I blame what happened next on adoption hormones (I swear there's such a thing). I wasn't pregnant, but my moods changed as quickly as the weather in Oklahoma.

"You're acting a little crazy about the crib," John said, irritated. "We have plenty of time to worry about this."

A few obscenities flew from my pretty mouth as I hurled a nearby book at his head. I cried. We both yelled. We quickly decided it was in the best interest of our marriage to close the office door, leave the junk piled on the floor, and deal with it on a day when my emotions weren't swirling like an F5 tornado.

From the time I was a small girl, decked out in a red leotard and twirling my baton in the front yard, I have *loved* to check the mail. It was (and still is, if I'm honest) a highlight of my day. In elementary school, I would greet the mailman each day, hoping he would hand me a letter from my pen pal, Carlye. These days, the mail consists mostly of bills and junk, but it's always fun to find a bright-colored envelope tucked between the electric and gas bills.

Besides my slight obsession with checking the mail (I tend to get mad if John checks it), I also love to send cards. I could spend hours perusing Hallmark, choosing the perfect card for a special occasion. Our bank account would probably be a little more padded if I didn't spend so much on stamps.

I waited anxiously for our CIS approval letter. Each day, as I drove home from work, my excitement would build at the thought of the letter waiting for me in the mailbox, the last piece of our dossier puzzle. I'd pull into the garage, throw my car into park, swing open the door, and walk quickly (or run) to the mailbox, praying I'd find the letter mixed in with the usual bills and credit card offers.

The door of the mailbox would creak as I opened it, only to find that the letter hadn't been delivered. I'd drag myself inside, throw the pile of unwanted mail on the kitchen table, and sulk.

Even the Easter cards didn't elicit the joy they normally did. I was stalking my mailbox, waiting on one single letter.

It was the first time during our adoption process that I grew completely impatient. I feared the worst. What if our letter had gotten lost? I wrestled with anxiety over a silly piece of paper, but that letter was the key to getting to Ethiopia. *Please, please, Mr. Postman. Deliver my letter soon.*

I stalked my mailbox day in and day out for four weeks before the letter finally arrived.

I checked the mail early that day because it had been raining and our mailbox tends to leak. I didn't want a bunch of soggy mail, and I especially didn't want a soggy approval letter if it happened to be waiting for me.

The mailbox squeaked as I opened it. On top of the stack sat the letter I had been waiting twenty-eight days for, and it was dry.

I rushed inside and ripped open the envelope. My heart sank at the sight of the pink piece of paper. Had we been denied? Some friends of ours had problems with their I-600A, and I feared we hadn't been cleared. Confused, I began reading the letter, still unsure if it was the approval I'd been waiting for. In complete panic and on the verge of tears, I called Kathleen.

"Read the letter to me," she said.

I began reading, and before I could finish, Kathleen exclaimed, "You've been approved!"

It took me a moment to wrap my mind around what she was saying. We were approved? Relief washed over me, and I shared my excitement with my friend. The pink slip of paper was a reminder that our approval was only good for one year. As I read the letter in more detail, I noticed that we were officially approved on April 20, 2011. My sister's birthday!

With the letter in my hand, all that kept us from being placed on the official wait list was a notary.

After six intense months of paperwork, a home study, fingerprint appointments, doctor appointments, and everything in between, we officially became a waiting family on April 29, 2011. I couldn't think of a better early Mother's Day gift. We had made it to the point in our journey where everything was completely out of our hands. All we could do was wait.

At the time we were placed on the wait list, we had raised $20,645, $7,000 shy of being fully funded. We had fund-raised nonstop since July, and I felt that God was asking me to rest. I believed John and I were supposed to take a break and trust that He would provide the additional money we needed when the time came for us to board a plane to Ethiopia. I had witnessed God provide more than $20,000, yet I doubted His ability to provide the remaining funds we needed to get to Ethiopia. After seeing the incredible ways the Lord had provided, you would think I would have been confident that He would take care of the rest. But I wasn't. I wanted to be in control. I wanted to have a plan and know for certain where the remaining money would come from. I needed to be doing something, but God whispered, "Be still, and know that I am God" (Psalm 46:10).

One morning as I got ready for work, God confirmed what I had been feeling in my spirit through the Christian radio station I was listening to. No more fund-raising.

"Jesus will meet your need as the need arises," the DJ said.

I stopped curling my hair, fumbled for a pen and my journal, and scribbled the words across a clean page. It was ridiculous to think God would provide all of our agency fees and then leave us hanging when the time came to travel to get our child. I had to remember that "my God [would] supply [my] every need according to His glorious riches in Christ Jesus" (Philippians 4:19).

CHAPTER 6

Temptation Strikes

Whether you turn to the right or to the left, your ears will hear a voice behind you saying, "This is the way; walk in it."

—ISAIAH 30:21

We had been on the wait list exactly one month when our agency reported it would be at least eighteen months before we received a referral. As the wait time increased and more families withdrew from the Ethiopia program, the Devil began playing tricks with my head. A part of me celebrated when each family left the program because it meant we moved up a step on the wait list. But as I rejoiced, I also became bitter. How could these families give up so easily? There were so many children who needed forever families. How could they walk away without a fight?

One minute I felt complete peace about our decision to wait things out, and the next I doubted everything. A thousand questions swirled through my mind. Are we supposed to go a different direction? Am I really hearing God correctly? Am I praying enough? Is my faith strong enough?

I hated the Devil and his sneaky tactics.

God had changed the course for many families (including some we knew), but I still pictured the faces of five million Ethiopian orphans who deserved to be adopted just as much as any other orphan. My heart ached; it grieved me to think of not adopting from Ethiopia. We didn't want to step outside of God's will for us and change the entire course of our adoption simply because we were impatient. John and I decided that unless the Ethiopia program completely shut down or God gave us a very big sign, we would forge ahead. We wanted to be obedient to what God had called us to do, even if the timetable wasn't what we had hoped.

The book *Sun Stand Still* is based on Joshua's bold prayer found in Joshua 10:12. He dared to ask God for the impossible. "O sun, stand still over Gibeon, O moon, over the Valley of Aijalon." Joshua needed God to intervene in a big way so he could fulfill God's promise to him. And God did. He literally made the sun stand still. "The sun stopped in the middle of the sky and delayed going down for a full day. There has never been a day like it before or since ... surely the LORD was fighting for Israel" (vv. 13–14). Author Steven Furtick dared readers to begin praying *Sun Stand Still* prayers, boldly asking God to do the impossible in their lives.

If God could make the sun stand still for Joshua, surely He could soften the hearts of government officials in Ethiopia. I wanted to have the kind of faith that believed God could answer my *Sun Stand Still* prayers. As the months passed, and we continued to wait, I reminded myself of something else Furtick wrote, "The darker it gets, the brighter our faith can shine."[1]

Several of our friends left the Ethiopia program to pursue Congolese adoptions. I was intrigued when I discovered there was a need for families to adopt from the Congo with shorter wait times and only one required trip to the country. Without praying about it, I decided to look into the Congo program.

I was quickly sucked into the excitement and new possibilities. Before I realized it, I was chasing paperwork again and crunching numbers to see if we could financially swing leaving the Ethiopia program to pursue a Congolese adoption. I was so busy trying to figure out the logistics that I ignored the huge knot in the pit of my stomach.

I called our social worker to inform her that we would likely be leaving the Ethiopia program and turned in the initial application to the agency associated with the Congo program. I mailed requests for marriage licenses and birth certificates. However, with each step I completed, my anxiety only intensified.

John and I researched the Congo and came across some disturbing travel advisories posted by the US government. We both had a sick feeling, and my stomach twisted like a pretzel. The Holy Spirit was trying to tell me I was on the wrong path. I had taken things into my own hands and left God out. And being outside of God's will was a scary place to be.

Despite the late hour, I called our social worker in a panic and left a desperate message. "We do *not* want to leave the program," I said. "Please do not close our file. Can you call me first thing in the morning?" I prayed she hadn't begun the process of closing our file. I lay in bed, unable to sleep, plagued with worry.

The next morning, my phone rang. I felt an instant wave of peace wash over me the moment our social worker explained that nothing had changed with our status. I was so thankful for God's grace.

For the first time since looking into the Congo program, I felt peace. There were no neon signs telling us to switch to the Congo or to stay with the Ethiopia program. Sometimes, I wish there had been. Furtick wrote, "You may be under the illusion that when God ignites great things in your life, He'll announce it with a big bang. He might. It's more likely that He won't. So stop waiting around for the big bang. Pay attention to the subtle clues and the still, small voice."[2]

All I had to guide me was the peace I felt about Ethiopia and the dread I felt chasing after a Congolese adoption.

It had been an emotional day. At any given point, I felt I would cry. Finally, I had to get up from my desk and take a walk because the tears just sprang forth, uninvited.

Choosing daily to persevere and continue on the path God had chosen for me on when others were going in a thousand different directions was difficult. Watching our friends, who we thought would travel to Ethiopia with us, change programs made me sad. The reality was they would likely receive a referral much sooner than we would, and that made me envious. I felt very alone.

The unexpected changes in the adoption world were taking a toll on me. The Devil was doing all he could to plant seeds of doubt in my mind and make me question if I had heard God correctly.

After feeling out of sorts all day, I was eager to get to my weekly women's Bible study. We had started a short Beth Moore study, and I wasn't a bit surprised when God met me exactly where I needed.

Those who know me well, or who have read my blog for

very long, know that Beth Moore rocks my socks off. There is just something about her Texas twang and her love for Jesus that makes me want to soak up every word of her teaching. That particular night, her words were powerful. It was like God was shouting, "Jennifer, Jennifer, don't miss this!"

Beth said, "God has made a promise over your life, and He will fulfill it! But until you put your feet on your Promised Land, the Devil has his all over it."

I couldn't keep the tears from falling. God had pointed John and me to what we believed was our Promised Land, and the Devil was doing all he could to keep us out of it. As we studied Scripture in the first chapter of Joshua, verse three grabbed my attention: "I will give you every place where you set your foot."

Beth said, "We receive this promise when we act; when we step out in faith." I immediately scribbled her words next to the verse in my Bible. She continued with Joshua 3:15. "Now the Jordan is at flood stage all during the harvest. Yet as soon as the priests who carried the ark reached the Jordan and their feet touched the water's edge, the water from upstream stopped flowing." Next to that verse I wrote, "God will part the waters for us, but we have to be willing to get our feet wet."

I couldn't allow fear to rob me of my Promised Land. I had to put my faith in the same God who promised Joshua (despite his fears) that he would cross the Jordan River into his Promised Land. Time and time again, God told Joshua, "Be strong and very courageous. Do not be terrified; do not be discouraged" (Joshua 1:9).

I'm sure the Devil messed with Joshua's head just as much as he messed with mine. Yet Joshua stood firm and chose to believe God, unmoved by fear.

I was so thankful for the women in my Bible study. The majority of them were older than me by at least ten years, but the age difference didn't keep us from bonding on a deep, spiritual level.

I cherished their wisdom, encouragement, prayers, and support throughout our adoption.

I had the privilege of studying the Bible with Kim, one of my dearest friends, her mother, and her grandmother. Three generations of amazing Christian women who loved the Lord and were dedicated to lifting our adoption and me up in prayer. They had been praying for my future children long before adoption became our plan. They were there through the infertility. They were there when God first placed Ethiopia on my heart. They stood in the gap for me during the many ups and downs.

The same night we studied Joshua overcoming fear to reach his Promised Land, I shared my own fears with my friends. I admitted how hard it was to stay on the path God had for me when so many others were going in different directions, and how desperately I wanted to be faithful to God's calling for my life.

Encouragement and affirmation flowed from their lips. They agreed that God had brought me to this place and wouldn't forsake me. They encouraged me to press on and keep my eyes on Jesus. And they prayed.

That night as I drove home, I heard these beautiful lyrics by Laura Story on the radio:

> We doubt your goodness, we doubt your love
> As if every promise from your Word is not enough
> All the while, You hear each desperate plea
> And long that we have faith to believe.[3]

That song was a reminder that even in the darkest situations, those times when you have no idea how things are going to turn out, God is faithful.

—⊷⊶—

The warm sand slid between my toes, the smell of salt filled the air, and the sound of the crashing waves calmed my anxious heart. I opened my devotion and read:

> Many voices will clamor for your attention, trying to divert you to another path. I have called each of My children to a different path, distinctly designed for that one. Do not let anyone convince you that his path is the only right way. And be careful not to extol your path as superior to another's way.[4]

I looked out over the vast Atlantic Ocean and realized that I couldn't be upset with those who had chosen to leave the Ethiopia program. God's plan for their future family was different than His plan for mine.

That was just one example of many during our weeklong trip to Florida that God confirmed in my heart that I was on the right path. There were no burning bushes, and I didn't hear God's audible voice, but through several books I was reading, God filled me with a peace that only comes from Him.

> Not only do you need to believe in God's ability to bring you across the Jordan, but you also need to trust him enough to let him develop a heart of sacrifice and surrender inside of you. It's tempting to want to skip right to the sun-stopping,

river-crossing stuff—the increased influence, answered prayers, and electrifying experiences of God's presence. But that stuff won't be genuine and certainly can't be sustained if it isn't cultivated out of a heart that has been formed by the spirit of God. Before God can bring His promises to pass in your life, He has to strip away all the stuff that keeps you from trusting Him wholeheartedly … When what you see around you doesn't match up with what God has spoken inside you, you've got to hold on to what you've heard. Paul said it best in 2 Corinthians 5:7 "We live by faith, not by sight."[5]

CHAPTER 7

Giving Me Eyes to See

Once our eyes are opened, we can't pretend we
don't know what to do. God, who weighs our
hearts and keeps our souls, knows what we know,
and holds us responsible to act.
—PROVERBS 24:12

A s I drove to work, I prayed that God would change me.
I sensed transformation occurring in my heart and saw
a glimpse of who He wanted me to be. I asked Him to
take me outside my comfort zone, to allow me to be His hands
and feet. I believed He wanted more for my life than simply
motherhood and was using our adoption to reveal His plans to
me. He wanted to mold me into a woman who reflected more of
His image for the world to see.

Until that point, my heart had been hardened toward the poor.
The poverty that ravaged Third World countries never crossed my
mind before we opened our hearts to an orphan living in those
horrific conditions. God began breaking my heart for the millions of
people around the world who live without clean drinking water, who
die from preventable diseases, and who live on two dollars or less a day.

Without judgment, He exposed my sinful heart. I relied too much on money. I was too comfortable. My security came from my bank account, not from the only One who would never fail me. God opened my eyes to see the world beyond Oklahoma, beyond the United States, and, most important, beyond my own selfishness.

Author Francis Chan, in his book *Crazy Love,* dares Christians to live their lives by placing their trust in God instead of money or material things. I desperately wanted to live my life desiring more of Jesus and less of worldly things. Chan wrote, "What is more messed up—that we have so much compared to everyone else, or that we don't think we're rich? That on any given day we might flippantly call ourselves 'broke' or 'poor.' We are neither of these things. We are rich. Filthy rich ... Being rich is a serious disadvantage spiritually because prosperity hardens the heart."[1] I was being challenged to desire God more than financial security. Chan writes,

> Lukewarm Christians do not live by faith—their lives are structured so they never have to. They don't have to trust God if something unexpected happens—they have their savings account. They don't need God to help them—they have their retirement plan in place. They don't genuinely seek out what life God would have them live— they have life figured out and mapped out. They don't depend on God on a daily basis—their fridge is stocked and for the most part, they are in good health. The truth is, their lives wouldn't look much different if they suddenly stopped believing God.[2]

It's so easy to get caught up in what the world says you need to have—a size-six body, the trendiest clothes, a bigger house, and a new car. Our adoption put the world-pleasing side of me in the spotlight.

"Lord, you're calling John and me to adopt a child from a country where people live on less than a dollar a day," I prayed. "Kids are starving. Help me get a grip! Strip away every single desire I have for more stuff. You are more than enough."

While I stand in front of a fully stocked refrigerator and complain that nothing looks good, people all across the world are digging through garbage to find their next meal. Older orphans often look on as their tummies growl as the ones get to eat, simply because there's not enough food to go around. Every forty-five seconds a child in Africa dies of malaria, which can be prevented by a six-dollar mosquito net according to Nothing But Nets, the global, grassroots campaign that raises awareness and money to fight the leading cause of death among African children. I'm considered rich because I have a roof over my head, clothes on my back, food in my fridge, and access to medical care. I was selfish to think I deserved more.

The Bible says we're not to store up "treasures on earth, but instead we are to store up treasures in heaven" (Matthew 6:19). We are also commanded to be content as long as we have food and clothing (1 Timothy 6:8). But our society portrays a completely different picture than God's Word, and it's when we start living by the world's standards that we get into trouble. Take it from someone who racked up $15,000 in credit card debt in her early twenties because she was deceived into thinking the things of the world could fill the void that only Jesus could. With just one trip to the mall, I would get sucked into the lie that I needed some name-brand clothes because they would make me look and feel good, which would ultimately make me happy.

I was about to bring home a child who may or may not have

food and clothing, and I was *still* allowing the Devil to fool me into thinking that I had to keep up with the world's standards.

But God is clear. He says, "Do not conform any longer to the pattern of this world, but be transformed by the renewing of your mind. Then you will be able to test and approve what God's will is—his good, pleasing, and perfect will" (Romans 12:2). There's a constant war raging between my flesh and my spirit. My biggest fear is that I'll be fighting the battle over my desire for material things until the day I die, and I hate that about myself.

In the Bible study *No Other Gods*, Author Kelly Minter shared an e-mail from a friend and former missionary in China. Her friend wrote the following after returning to the United States:

> If it be any encouragement to you all, this is what I saw, especially in America: pain (deep, private, unanticipated, suffocating) met with stubborn hope (white-knuckled, clinging to Him, rock-bottom conviction that His offer of Reconciliation is the only viable option, and a willingness to risk believing that Redemption is not only something that means we get to go to heaven, but something that He is passionate to carry out now, in specific life situations, to make things show His brand of beauty—in which a healed relationship or person can reflect more glory than one who never knew brokenness).[3]

Minter added how she longed to become "a person who is clinging to God with fierce abandon despite my caving and pained heart, believing indeed that 'redemption is not only something that means I get to go to heaven, but something that He is passionate to carry out now.'"[4] God had redeemed me and promised me eternity with Him, but I wanted Him to release me from the death grip the world had on me.

———— ∞ ————

Early in our adoption process, when thousands of dollars still loomed over our heads, I remember praying, "God, I think it pretty much sucks that so much money stands in the way of children having families." The emotions behind that prayer stemmed from a story I had read about a family from Texas who had left everything they loved behind to move to Haiti. A lump formed in my throat, and I fought back tears as I read about the family who had sacrificed comfort and the American dream to offer hope to people in desperate need of it.

We live in a fallen world where so many people's basic needs go unmet. But more than needing food and clothing, these individuals need to hear that they are loved. They need to know there is hope. They need someone to tell them how much Jesus loves them.

A Haitian woman had begged and pleaded with the family from Texas to take her four-week-old baby because she couldn't care for it. But because of strict Haitian adoption laws, the family couldn't take the baby, and she ended up in an orphanage. When the family visited the orphanage, they found the baby lying on a dirt floor, sucking her fingers in an attempt to soothe herself as tears rolled down her dirty cheeks. She was covered in spit-up. "While many American churches are worrying about lighting on their stage, or fussing over the displays in their foyer, children are suffering in orphanages, groaning, aching, for someone to come redeem their lives,"[5] the family shared on their blog.

As I allowed myself to get lost in the baby girl's chocolate-colored eyes—eyes filled with so much sadness—my heart shattered. I ached at the thought of our child yearning for someone to love him or her. The Haitian baby in the photo on my computer screen could have been our child.

Not everyone is called to adopt a child, but every Christian is called to do something. When we see the face of a child in need, we aren't supposed to turn our heads, close our eyes, and forget. God holds us responsible to act.

I have a dream … that little black boys and little black girls will be able to join hands with little white boys and white girls as brothers and sisters.

—Martin Luther King, Jr.

Until I envisioned my family portrait including a white mother and father loving and raising black children, I never acknowledged Martin Luther King Jr. Day. It had just been another day that I didn't have to go to work or school.

I personally saw nothing wrong with the family portrait God was painting, yet I knew I was still very much the minority. In the small Texas town where I was raised, the majority of families were white. International adoption wasn't common, and families didn't cross racial lines. When people questioned John's and my decision to adopt a black child, I realized how much prejudice still existed in the world.

I would have been naive to think that we wouldn't encounter criticism. Any God-sized dream comes with opposition. I had to be prepared for those who would stare and ask inappropriate questions once we brought our baby home. I prayed that I would handle any negativity with grace. I wanted to extend the same mercy toward people who criticized us as God had extended to me as He revealed the prejudice that had once resided in my own heart. A song I sang as a child in Sunday school came to mind as I prayed.

> Jesus loves the little children,
> all the children of the world.
> Red and yellow, black and white,
> they are precious in His sight.
> Jesus loves the little children of the world.[6]

When we thought of our Ethiopian child, we didn't see a color. We saw a child God had chosen for our family before the creation of the world.

A few days later as I drove home, a thought crossed my mind that almost caused me to slam on the brakes. I finally understood. Had I gotten pregnant when I wanted to, if God had answered my pleading prayers, I would have remained the same self-centered person. But God loved me so much that He wouldn't leave me wallowing in my sin.

God promises "that in all things God works for the good of those who love him, who have been called according to his purpose. For those God foreknew, he also predestined to be conformed to the likeness of his son" (Romans 8:28–29). Through my tears, I thanked God for seeing beyond my old self and not allowing me to stay comfortable and unchanged. In that moment, I knew I wouldn't have changed a single thing about my journey to become a mom.

God had opened my eyes to the world around me. He had given me a heart for Ethiopia, adoption, and the orphaned.

My infertility had a purpose far beyond what I could see or comprehend. It took God shaking up my world and taking my eyes off the negative pregnancy tests to realize it. I was reminded, yet again, of Joseph's response to his brothers' betrayal. "And now, do not be distressed and do not be angry at yourselves for selling me here because it was to save lives that God sent me ahead of you … so then, it was not you who sent me here, but God" (Genesis 45:5, 8). God allowed Joseph to be sold into slavery because there was an eternal purpose at stake. Despite the hopelessness I had felt, I knew God had an eternal purpose in mind for me too. I was aware of some of those purposes, but there were many I wouldn't understand this side of heaven. John and I weren't going to solve the world's orphan crisis, but we could make a difference in the life of one orphan.

Jesus wants us to take the gospel to the nations.

> Then the eleven disciples went to Galilee, to the mountain where Jesus had told them to go. When they saw him, they worshiped him; but some doubted. Then Jesus came to them and said, "All authority in heaven and on earth has been given to me. Therefore go and make disciples of all nations, baptizing them in the name of the Father and of the Son and of the Holy Spirit, and teaching them to obey everything I have commanded you. And surely I am with you always, to the very end of the age." (Matthew 28:16–20)

John and I would share the love of Jesus with one child—something he or she might never hear if he or she remained in an orphanage on the other side of the world. And we could be an example to others of how God wants us to open our hearts;

to stop looking at the color of someone's skin and love the way God commands us to love. Maybe others would step out of their comfort zones and choose to adopt, become foster parents, or simply support the global orphan crisis.

My prayer became that our adoption would have an eternal impact on our friends and family who had never given their life to Jesus Christ. God's glory weaved through our entire story, and I believed He could use it to turn the hardest heart toward the Savior. God uses the ordinary and the unlikely, walking in obedience to fulfill His purposes. He used Joseph's slavery, and I prayed He would use our adoption too.

Katie Davis moved to Uganda at eighteen years old and became the mother of more than a dozen Ugandan girls. Her story is inspiring. Her book *Kisses from Katie* touched my heart and challenged me, but one particular story impacted me the most.

She described an area of Uganda where the words *poor, poverty,* and *starvation* are an understatement. Women, desperate to feed their children, are forced into prostitution and other unfathomable situations. She wrote,

> Elizabeth, whose husband left her after her third child was born, had recently taken in her sister's five children after her sudden death. "What was my choice?" she asked when explaining the situation to me. "God says I look after orphans, I look after orphans." Elizabeth and the eight children sleep together on the floor in a home about half the size of my kitchen table.[7]

This Ugandan woman had nothing, yet she obeyed God's call to care for the orphans. We have everything, yet we ignore it and pretend it's not our problem. As Christians, caring for the poor and the orphan isn't negotiable. God is clear that we are to extend a hand to the poor, the orphan, and the widow. James 1:27 says, "Religion that God our Father accepts as pure and faultless is this: to look after orphans and widows in their distress and to keep oneself from being polluted by the world." God is calling us to action.

Too often, we sit in our comfy church pews, talking about how we're going to be the hands and feet of Jesus, yet we never do anything.

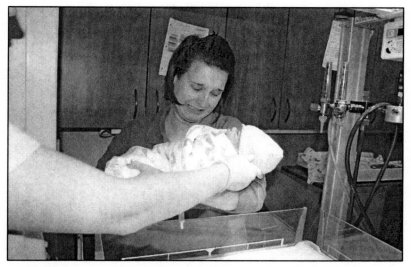

Holding my son for the first time just moments after he was born.
December 14, 2011.

Our first family photo!
December 14, 2011.

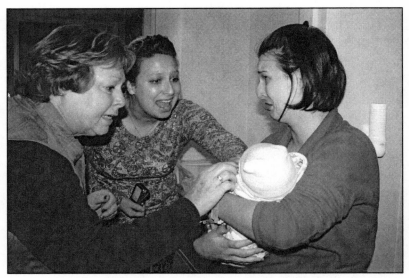

My mom (Lolli) and sister (Auntie M) meeting Jackson for the first time. There wasn't a dry eye. We had truly witnessed a miracle. December 14, 2011.

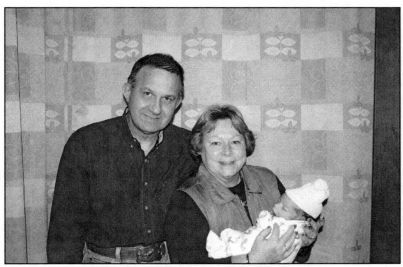

Pop and Lolli holding their first grandchild.

One of my favorite photos of John with our son.

Auntie M holding her nephew, who she likes to call
Jackson Henry or sometimes just Henry.

One of Jackson's newborn photos taken when he was one week old.
Photo courtesy of Casey Linde.

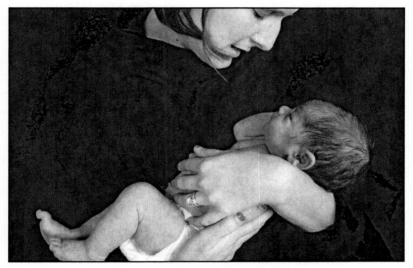

Mommy and her Little Man.
Photo courtesy of Casey Linde.

John's parents (Missy and Dude) meeting Jackson for the first time.

John's sister (Aunt Adrienne) meeting Jackson for the first time.

Autry was so excited to finally meet Jackson on Christmas
Eve 2011. She fed and held him for two hours.

With our friends Kathleen and Lyla. Kathleen and I prayed and encouraged each other through the long adoption process. Lyla was born one month after Jackson. They will always share a special bond.

Jackson's first trip to Saint Louis to visit John's family in February 2012.

Happy Gotcha Day, Jackson!
April 30, 2012.

Our wonderful friends Justin and Jessica helped
us celebrate Jackson's Gotcha Day!

Our families came to Oklahoma to celebrate Jackson's
Gotcha Day and his dedication at church.

Celebrating my mom being cancer free! Jackson wore
a special shirt that said, "I walk for Lolli" during the
2012 Relay for Life in Stephenville, Texas.

Spending the day at the Saint Louis Zoo with Missy and Dude.
May 2012.

Big Dude and Little Dude lounging at the lake. June 2012.

Our little Pooh Bear celebrating his first Halloween.
Photo courtesy of Casey Linde.

Our family on Orphan Sunday at my parents' church
in Texas. I was honored to share our adoption story
and bring awareness to the global orphan crisis.
November 2012.

Celebrating Thanksgiving with my family.
November 2012.

The photo we chose for our 2012 Christmas card.
Photo courtesy of Mylissa Parham.

Justin and Jessica came to visit in April 2013. No matter how
many miles separate us, Jackson never forgets them.

Jackson wearing a special shirt for his Pop.
Father's Day weekend 2013.

Autry and Jackson enjoying a Sprittle at Classic 50's
in Norman, Oklahoma. Autry comes to Oklahoma
each summer and spends a week with Jackson.
June 2013.

This smile is contagious! At eighteen months
old, he keeps us on our toes.

Our family during a visit to my parents' house in Texas.
June 2013.

Jackson with his Pop and Lolli during a visit to Texas.
June 2013.

CHAPTER 8

A Prayer Changes Everything

Today, if you hear his voice, do not harden your hearts.

—HEBREWS 4:7

In my Bible next to Hebrews 4:7, I wrote, "If God's calling you to do something, obey!" I listed the areas where God was calling me to action: adoption, a possible career in ministry, writing a book about our adoption journey, and living a more radical life for Him.

The item on my list that confused me was a career in ministry. I didn't have a theology degree, and I had no desire to go back to school to get one. God was challenging me to work in an area outside journalism and public relations.

I hated my current job. I sat at a small desk, in silence, five days a week, and was miserable. I needed to interact with people. While I loved writing, I wasn't fond of ghostwriting, especially books about Jesus and vampires (I'm not even kidding). I couldn't get the idea of a job in ministry out of my mind.

As I drove to work one morning, dreading the day ahead, I asked God to lead me to a job that had meaning. I wanted to use my gifts to serve Him. "Lord, I want to serve You. I have this deep desire to work in ministry, but I have no idea what that even looks like. I feel like You're asking me to step out of my comfort zone to serve the least of these. I know that doesn't mean I have to move to Africa. I know there are people in my own community who need to know Your love. How can I serve the people in my own backyard?"

As I began searching for job opportunities, I remembered my pastor telling me about openings at the local homeless shelter. I decided to e-mail another church member who worked there, and before I could think twice, I had submitted my résumé and had an interview scheduled. One week later, a job offer was on the table. Just weeks after uttering my prayer, God showed me exactly where He wanted me to work.

City Rescue Mission has served the homeless and near homeless in the Oklahoma City metro area for more than fifty years. The largest homeless shelter in Oklahoma, the mission houses the largest free drug-and-alcohol recovery program. Through its faith-based recovery program, thousands of men, women, and children have heard the good news of Jesus Christ. Lives have literally been saved through the compassionate, humanitarian services the mission provides to those in desperate need.

From the moment I stepped through the doors of City Rescue Mission, I was in awe of how God had orchestrated my being there. I even wondered if God would use the mission to fulfill my longing to be a mother.

The clients and staff started each day together in chapel. One of my first mornings, a coworker leading devotions said, "God has a purpose for your being exactly where you are." I had no idea just how true that statement was and all God had in store for me through my new job.

———— ⊗⊗⊗ ————

Part of my job description was to give the morning devotion at least once a month. The first time, I was excited but also nervous to stand in front of one hundred women and share what God was doing in my life. I could have easily just read the devotion and left it at that, but I felt God was answering another one of my prayers. I wanted to share John's and my story. I wanted people to see the hope we had in the midst of suffering, and I wanted to give God the glory. That morning, God spoke to the deep places of my heart through the devotion. He didn't use me to teach the women at the mission as much as He used them to teach me.

Although I hesitated at times, I decided I was going to be transparent with the women when I stood before them. I wasn't going to put a smile on my face and pretend my life was free from trials or that I was perfect.

The women living at the mission had arrived with a trunk load of baggage, but they weren't afraid to share their problems. They were real and transparent about the challenges they faced.

As I worked to prepare my devotions each month, God never failed to call me out of my comfort zone and stretch my faith.

"Do I really have to share that, God?" I would argue. "What will they think of me?" But God wanted me to be transparent, to share the pain of infertility, my unfulfilled longing to be a mother, and how He was transforming me through our adoption process.

After the last worship song ended, I made my way to the front of the room. I grabbed the microphone and checked to see that it was on. "Good morning, ladies," I said. I was shaking and the paper in my hands trembled. "Today's verse is Proverbs 3:5–6,

'Trust in the LORD with all your heart; don't try to figure out everything on your own. Listen to God's voice … in everything you do, everywhere you go; He's the one who will keep you on track.' As I read this verse, I was reminded of two things that I often forget when God's asking me to trust Him. First, I don't need to try to figure things out on my own. Second, when we put our trust in God, we can't indulge in human reasoning."

Someone hollered "Amen!" from the back of the room.

"It seems like a no-brainer to put our complete trust in God," I said. "After all, it's the basis of the Christian faith, but it's not always as easy as it seems."

I shared with the women that through our adoption I had learned to trust God on a completely new level. First, I had to trust that He would provide the money we needed to adopt. And second, I had to make a daily choice to trust Him regarding the hold-ups in Ethiopia. Then I went on to admit something I had never voiced.

"Even though God has provided in amazing ways for our adoption, I still find myself doubting how we'll come up with the seven thousand dollars we need to travel to Ethiopia. I've seen God provide twenty thousand dollars, but I still doubt," I said. "Many of you have been redeemed from lives of addiction, but you doubt God would use you for something great. We may come from different backgrounds, but doubt bonds us. When doubt hangs like a gray cloud above us, we have to remember who delivered us in the past."

As I walked to my office after devotions one morning, a hand grabbed me and pulled me away from the crowd. One of our clients who I had never met asked if she could pray for me.

"I was really touched by your devotion on doubt earlier in the week," she said. "I believe God will answer your prayers for a child very soon."

I sat down beside her, and she took my hands in hers and prayed one of the most beautiful prayers I had ever heard. "Lord, please provide the resources Jennifer needs for the adoption. Remove any obstacles that stand in her way of bringing children home from Ethiopia."

When she finished praying, she looked me in the eyes and continued holding my hand.

"Get the nursery ready," she said. "I feel in my spirit that you could have a baby very soon."

I fought back tears as I thanked her. I was humbled by the prayer she had uttered on behalf of my future children. A homeless woman living in a shelter who I had never spoken to until that morning had prayed the most dynamic, faith-filled prayer for me. I didn't know her story, but I was almost certain she was facing her own Goliaths—probably much larger than what I faced. Yet she had chosen to set her problems aside, obey God, and, through prayer, stand in agreement with me.

I hugged her and walked to my office. Then I realized I still didn't know her name.

God soothed my aching heart by allowing me to be a mother figure to many of the children who lived at the shelter. At the time, sixty children lived at the mission, the most there had ever been at one time.

Not long after I started the job, I met a three-year-old African American boy and his one-year-old sister. They captured my heart. Each morning, they greeted me with smiles and giggles and high fives. They would crawl into my lap during devotions and most days fell asleep in my arms. As I cuddled those babies, I got a glimpse of what my life would look like once our child was home. God filled my empty arms while I waited.

The kids lived at the mission with their grandmother. I hated the circumstances that had brought them there and was saddened that it was unlikely to get better for them.

I had never been flipped off by a three-year-old until I worked at the mission and didn't know the F-word could be part of the vocabulary of someone so young. My little friends needed love and a few good role models. Their situation made me question God. Why was it so hard for John and me to become parents when so many children were living without the love and stability they deserved? Every day I witnessed kids being pushed aside by their parents like an afterthought. They were nothing more than a nuisance to them. If I could have taken those children home, I would have.

They became the highlight of my day. I looked forward to the morning cuddles and afternoon visits at my desk. I never dreamed the day would come when I would have to tell them good-bye.

Their grandmother had nowhere to go, but she was determined she wasn't going to stay at the shelter any longer. She was tired of following rules. I watched as she packed up their belongings and prepared to leave with the babies I had grown to love so much.

John happened to be at the mission that afternoon as I told the kids good-bye. He held the little boy who was proud to be wearing his tie. I hugged the little girl tight, not wanting to let her go. I choked back tears, willing myself not to cry in front of them. They didn't know that the little stability they had was about to be taken from them. Their world was about to be turned upside down.

The little boy gave me one last high five as I squeezed his sister for the last time. Then I watched as they walked out the door and out of my life forever. My heart shattered, and I cried all the way home. Through those two precious kids, God showed me I was capable of loving children, no matter the color of their skin, as if they were my own.

***

Thankfully, my lap and heart didn't remain empty.

One morning, four-year-old Luke ran over to my desk and noticed the package of Special K cereal. I planned on eating it for breakfast but couldn't help but notice how much Luke seemed to want it.

"What's that Jennifer?" he asked, grabbing the plastic bag.

"It's cereal," I answered.

"Can I have some cereal, Jennifer?"

How could I resist his begging blue eyes? I handed him my breakfast, and he hugged me.

"Thank you, Jennifer," he said as he ran off grinning from ear to ear. You would have thought I had given him an all-access pass to Chucky Cheese.

The next morning during chapel, Luke tugged at my shirt. "Did you bring cereal today?" he smiled.

"Come to my desk after chapel, and I'll give you some," I said.

And that became our morning routine. Luke would come to my desk, and I would hand him a bag of cereal. And every morning, he was just as happy and thankful as he had been the first time I handed over my breakfast.

***

Loving Luke and the younger kids came easy for me. All I had to do was color with them, hold them, or bring them cereal. But it was the teenagers who challenged me. Their stories broke my heart. They had faced things no child should. I often felt helpless because I didn't have the answers or the ability to make things better for them. They needed more than a bag of bright-colored, fruit-flavored cereal.

I signed up to mentor one of the teenagers at the mission and was paired with Jamie, a sixteen-year-old who lived with her mom, older sister, and younger brother. She was having trouble in school, doubted if God existed, and told me she felt worthless and unwanted.

As we sat in my office getting to know one another, I couldn't believe the things she shared with me. She had experienced so much pain in such a short time. She believed her mother didn't love her as much as her siblings because she was the result of a one-night stand.

"Lord, what do I say to her," I silently pleaded. "You're going to have to give me the right words." I don't remember what I said to her that night, but as I drove home, God showed me exactly what I was supposed to do for Jamie through the words of a song by JJ Heller.

My heart was so burdened for Jamie. I wanted to do something to take her pain away, but God whispered, "Just love her."

Katie Davis, in her book *Kisses from Katie*, wrote,

> I felt deep in my spirit He was teaching me to care for the one person in front of me. I see thousands of deep brown eyes and feel thousands of little brown hands and I know that even on the hardest day, stopping is worth it. A life changed is worth

it, even if only one. God's love made known is
worth it, even if only for one. I will not save them
all. But I will keep trying. I will say "yes." I will
stop for one.[1]

There were days when I left work feeling like I had been
hit by a truck. Some days completely zapped me emotionally. I
worked with people who were hurting, desperate for love, and
struggling with addiction. I witnessed things that grieved my
heart in a way it had never before grieved. I carried the burdens
of so many people—especially the children who I had grown to
love. I began praying, "Lord, make me aware of the people you
place in front of me. Even if it's just one person who needs to feel
loved, show me who that one person is today."

When God asks us to be His hands and feet, it usually doesn't
mean we have to do extravagant things.

For I was hungry and you gave me something
to eat, I was thirsty and you gave me something
to drink, I was a stranger and you invited me in,
I needed clothes and you clothed me, I was sick
and you looked after me, I was in prison and you
came to visit me. Then the righteous will answer
"Lord, when did we see you hungry and feed
you, or thirsty and give you something to drink?
When did we see you a stranger and invite you
in, or needing clothing and cloth you? When
did we see you sick or in prison and go to visit
you?" The King will reply, "I tell you the truth,
whatever you did for one of the least of these
brothers of mine, you did for me." (Matthew
25:35–40)

For me, loving one meant stopping, even if I was extremely busy, to listen to a client at the mission and her dreams of helping sex-trafficking victims. It meant helping her research how to start a ministry at her church. Loving one meant holding K.K., one of the babies at the mission, during chapel, so her mom could have a break. Loving one meant handing out candy to the kids who bombarded my desk each day after school, eagerly awaiting their daily treat.

Loving one meant letting Luke crawl into my lap while I worked and answering his *many* questions and giving Mia a pen and paper so she could color beside me at my desk. Loving one meant cheering on a little boy with frail legs as he ran and tried his hardest to play hockey, never letting his disability slow him down.

Loving one meant praying for a little boy who I hoped, despite his parents constant screaming, knew how much Jesus loved him. Loving one meant tying a little girl's shoelaces when her mom was too busy and helping a client with her résumé so she could get a job and make a better life for her and her son. Loving one meant helping a mother get to Oklahoma City to be with her daughter during surgery.

Katie Davis said it best, "We aren't called to save the world, not even to save one person; Jesus does that. We are just called to love with abandon. We are called to enter into our neighbors' suffering and love them right there."[2]

CHAPTER 9

A Divine Detour

Let us hold unwavering to the hope we profess for
He who promised is faithful.
—HEBREWS 10:23

"Headed to lunch," I said as I grabbed my keys and phone from my desk. It was officially summer in Oklahoma, and my soul felt as parched as the flowers withering in my front yard. Like my begonias, which were desperate for a cool, steady, rain, I needed something to lift my spirits. We had only been on the wait list for three months, and it was already taking its toll on me. I hoped lunch with my friend Shelli would help brighten my mood.

"Dude, will you please return these calls for me?" Justin begged. He sat at the desk beside me, staring at the blinking red light on his phone. "Just calling cause I want to volunteer," he said, mocking the messages that awaited him.

"Nope, I'm not your secretary," I said, laughing at his on-the-spot imitation.

"Ugh!" he said, picking up the phone to make the dreaded calls.

Justin began working at the mission one month after I did. He strolled in wearing khakis, boat shoes, and a Mr. Rogers sweater. *Who is this guy?* I thought as I shook his hand that day.

Justin's knowledge of the Bible intimidated me, but I quickly discovered that we shared a passion for social justice—and that, despite his choice of attire, I was actually older than him. "So you're adopting from Africa?" he asked from across the breakroom table on his first day.

"Yep!" I said and told him every single detail of our story.

Justin and his wife, Jessica, became fast friends of John and me. The kind of friends that kick their shoes off at the front door, collapse on your couch, and call dibs on the remote.

"We can go for coffee this afternoon," I hollered over my shoulder as I walked toward the door.

"Sounds good," Justin said as he dialed the phone. "Later, dude!"

I heard someone call my name as I watched for Shelli out the window. I turned to see my coworker Tammy walking toward me. "Jennifer, do you have a minute?"

"Sure. I'm just waiting on a friend to pick me up for lunch."

"I know you are trying to adopt a baby from Africa, but one of our clients is pregnant and wants to place the baby for adoption. I thought you and John might be interested."

I couldn't believe what I was hearing.

"She's eighteen years old, and every day she tells me she has to find a family for her baby," Tammy said. "She wants to find an attorney and sign her rights away."

"I'll lose my job if I try to adopt a client's baby," I said. Questions swirled in my mind. There were a thousand reasons why John and I couldn't adopt that baby. First, she was a client. Second, we couldn't afford two adoptions. Third, I didn't know the first thing about pursuing a private, domestic adoption. Fourth, what if she changed her mind once the baby was born? Fifth, we were on the wait list for Ethiopia. And sixth, did I mention I could lose my job?

"Will you at least pray about it?" Tammy asked.

I agreed to pray and talk to John, but deep down I didn't see how it could work in our favor.

"I'll be praying too," Tammy said.

About that time, Shelli drove up. My head was spinning as I climbed into her car. "You're never going to believe what just happened," I said as we headed to the pizza joint around the block. "A coworker just asked if we wanted to adopt a client's baby."

"What??" Shelli squealed. "Did you say yes?"

"I told her it was crazy, that I'd get fired."

Then it suddenly hit me—the advice a friend and fellow adoptive mom had given me early in our adoption process. "Never put God in a box," she said. "He has a way of surprising you when you least expect it. He can bring your children from anywhere as long as your heart remains open."

For the rest of the day, thoughts of the client and her unborn child consumed my thoughts. I ignored the lingering urge to call John and share the news, deciding it was best to tell him in person, but I couldn't keep the secret.

"Want to grab coffee?" I asked Justin.

"Sure. You're driving."

Grabbing coffee was a daily occurrence, but Justin often opted for a Red Bull. My drink of choice, however, never changed—a large Dr. Pepper with extra ice. We went for "coffee" so often that Justin could order for me without having to ask what I wanted.

As we drove to the nearby convenient store, I told Justin about the baby.

"That's nuts," he said. "Who's the client?"

"I don't know her name. We'd be crazy to pursue this. Don't you think I'd get fired?"

"Possible."

"But even though I absolutely love my job, it would be worth it if it meant finally becoming a mom, right?"

"You can always find another job," he said.

My heart was burdened for the young girl living at a homeless shelter and facing the most difficult decision of her life. "Lord, please be with the girl living at the mission and her baby," I prayed. "Guide her as she makes such a big decision. I have no idea if we're supposed to adopt this baby. Give me wisdom to know what we're supposed to do. I trust that you'll make a way if it's meant to be."

I could hardly wait to tell John about my day. The thought of pursuing the adoption excited me. I was barely through the door before I bombarded him with the details. "So, Tammy had something pretty crazy to tell me today," I said.

"Really?" John said as he unpacked his lunch and put the dirty dishes in the sink.

"There's an eighteen-year-old living at the mission who wants to place her baby for adoption. Tammy wants to know if we'd be interested in adopting it."

"We're adopting from Ethiopia," John said without turning around.

"Yeah, I told her I'd probably lose my job if I tried to adopt a client's baby," I said, trying to hide my hurt from John's lack of excitement. "But I told her I'd pray about it. Will you at least pray about it?"

"Sure, but we can't afford two adoptions," John said as he walked toward our bedroom to change out of his work clothes.

I stood in the kitchen, trying not to show my frustration. What if God was opening a new door? John obviously didn't think so, but I wasn't giving up on the idea.

The following day, Tammy stopped by my desk to share a few more details. The birth mother was almost five months pregnant and was due in early December. She was also persistent. Just that morning, she had asked Tammy again if she knew a family who could adopt her baby.

I began feeling more and more that we were supposed to pursue the adoption. I called John and told him what Tammy had shared with me.

"I promise I'll pray about it," he said.

I needed to educate myself on the logistics of a private, domestic adoption. The domestic process was completely different than international. A friend had recommended an adoption attorney, who just so happened to attend our church. I gave her a call.

"We aren't certain we'll pursue adopting the baby," I told her. "But I wanted to find out what the process looked like."

"There are two things you need to keep in mind," she advised. "The birth mother can change her mind at any point until the baby is born. There's no way to hold her to her decision. Only when she hands the baby over and her rights have been terminated will it become final. You also need more information on the birth father. His rights have to be terminated too."

Two weeks had passed since God had thrown us a curve ball. I couldn't stop thinking about the birth mom and the well-being of her baby. I worried the birth father would refuse to sign his rights away and feared losing my job, but luckily, John was coming around to the crazy idea.

I needed to talk to the president of the mission about our plans to proceed with the adoption, but I feared the worst.

When I finally worked up the courage to talk to Tom, I was shocked when he gave me his blessing. There was just one catch: He would have to inform the board of our plans, and the members would have to approve it.

"Lord, please prepare the hearts of the board members," I prayed. "If this baby is supposed to be ours, please make a way. Let the board members see that John and I want nothing more than to love this baby as our own."

Deep in my spirit, I heard the familiar whisper. The same one that had promised to make me a mother through adoption the night I sat in a Mexican restaurant. "This is your child." And at that moment, I knew Christmas would come early at our house.

Two weeks had passed since God had thrown us a curve ball. I couldn't stop thinking about the birth mom and the well-being of her baby. I worried the birth father would refuse to sign his rights away and feared losing my job, but luckily, John was coming around to the crazy idea.

The birth mother, who I'll refer to as Allison, knew there was a couple praying about whether to adopt her baby. Tammy told her she needed to be confident with her decision before moving forward.

We knew as her pregnancy progressed, and the baby kicked

with more intensity, there was a chance Allison would decide to keep the baby. The last thing we wanted was for her to feel she couldn't change her mind.

I had spoken to Allison several times but had no reason to believe she knew I was the woman longing to be the mother of her child. One afternoon, she pulled up a chair and sat down across from Justin. Our desks were in the main lobby of the mission so we were used to clients stopping by to chat, a perk to sitting in the noisy lobby. I couldn't always hear the person I was on the phone with, but I was able to invest in the clients and get to know them on a deeper level.

Justin and I pushed our work aside and listened as Allison shared the unfortunate circumstances that had led her to the mission. I let Justin do the majority of the talking, as I wanted to soak up every word she said. If we ended up adopting her baby, I wanted to know as much as I could about the woman who had carried my child.

Allison was enrolled in the mission's Bridge to Life program. The recovery program helped clients identify the obstacles in their lives that had prevented them from overcoming cycles of dysfunction and equipped them to overcome those obstacles in the future.

"Do you plan to graduate from BTL?" Justin asked.

"Yes," she said. "I may have to take some time off to have the baby, but I won't need long."

"Why's that?" Justin asked.

"I'm not keeping the baby. Tammy says she knows a couple who may want to adopt it. I hope they do. I'm not responsible enough to be a mom."

I froze and avoided making eye contact with Allison. She was talking about me. I was sitting less than five feet from her, and she had no idea that I was the one who wanted to raise her child.

"Have you had any counseling to help you with this decision?" Justin asked. "It's a pretty big one."

"Some people at my church say I'm making the right decision," Allison said. "They say it's very selfless of me. I'm praying I don't form too much of a bond with the baby since I know I can't take care of it."

John and I were going to have to tell her we were the couple who wanted to adopt her child—and it needed to be sooner rather than later. We couldn't risk her finding out from someone other than us.

As Allison got up to go to her next class, I immediately dialed Tammy's extension. "I think it's time for us to tell her," I said.

Tammy arranged for John and me to sit down with Allison four days later. We were eager to tell her that we were the couple who wanted to adopt her child. One minute I was overcome with excitement and the next a bundle of nerves. It was a relief knowing things would be out in the open, but I was unsure what to say to the person who would give me the thing my heart most desired. I hadn't said anything the day Allison shared her adoption plan with Justin and me, and I didn't want her to feel she had been deceived.

John came to the mission as soon as he got off work. We sat at my desk and waited for Tammy and Allison. As they approached, a look of surprise and relief spread across Allison's face.

"You know Jennifer," Tammy said. "This is her husband, John, and they are the couple I've been telling you about."

"I kind of thought it might be you," Allison said with a smile. "I remember you talking about wanting to adopt kids during devotions."

Tammy led us to an empty room in the mission where we could talk in private. Only a handful of people knew of our plans to adopt Allison's baby, and we didn't want other clients becoming curious if they saw us meeting with her. John and I wanted to spend time getting to know our birth mother without interruptions and also wanted Allison to feel comfortable asking questions.

We sat opposite each other on bottom bunks in the hot and cramped sparse room. We were all unsure how to start the conversation, so I decided to go first. "I guess the first thing we want you to know is that we never want you to feel like you can't change your mind," I said. "If at any point you think you want to raise your child, you have to tell us. We won't be mad. Just be honest with us."

"I'm not going to change my mind," Allison said. "I'm not responsible enough to take care of a baby."

She was completely confident in her decision, not only for her child but also for herself.

"Is there anything you want to know about us?" John asked. We were surprised by some of her questions.

"So, John, what do you do for a living?" she asked.

"I'm a neuropsychologist at the VA," John said.

She nodded, satisfied with his career choice. "Will you be at the hospital with me when the baby is born?" she asked.

"If you want us to be there," I said. "Those are the kind of details we will have to work out with the attorney."

"Do you want an open or closed adoption?" she asked.

"Well, since we know each other, I think we'd be okay with an open adoption," I said.

"I don't want to see the baby during the first years because it needs to bond with you," she said. "It needs to know that you are its parents, but photos would be nice."

I bit my lip to keep from crying. I couldn't believe Allison had just referred to us as the parents of her child. We told her we would make an appointment with the adoption attorney and let her know what the next step would be.

"There is one thing we need to ask you," John said. "Do you know who the father is?"

"Yes, but I don't want to say who he is," she said. "I don't even know where he is."

"I think you're going to have to give the attorney his name," I said. "Legally, he has to sign his rights away too."

"Can't I just say I don't know who it is?" she asked.

"We can't lie," I said.

She wrung her hands, her expression one of dread.

"I have to believe God will honor the decision you've made for your baby," I continued. "We have to trust that He will work out the details with the birth father."

Allison didn't seem convinced that revealing the identity of the birth father was the best decision. We could persuade her to tell the truth, but we couldn't force her. I prayed she would make the right choice.

The meeting with Allison went better than we had hoped, but John and I were both apprehensive about the lack of information on the birth father. Once he discovered Allison was pregnant, he could refuse to terminate his rights. We feared that could lead to a messy custody battle.

I felt like David facing Goliath. And like David, I realized my only option was to use "the name of the Lord as my defense" (1 Samuel 17:45). I asked God to ease Allison's anxiety about the birth father. During my quiet time, God led me to 1 Peter 3:6, "Do what is right and do not give way to fear." And then there it was again. That still, small voice. "Why are you afraid? Your faith and hope is in Me, and I am much bigger than your fears." I scribbled the verse on a piece of paper and tucked it in my Bible.

The next morning, I called Allison over to my desk and handed her the piece of paper that contained God's promise. "I know you're afraid, but God has this," I said.

She unfolded the slip of paper, read the verse, and gave me the birth father's name.

In late August, John and I were finally ready to tell our parents that Santa would be bringing them their first grandchild!

I was excited to share our news with my parents, but I was also nervous. Their initial reaction to our Ethiopian adoption wasn't exactly warm and fuzzy. Our international adoption rarely came up in conversation, so I was surprised when my mom asked if we had been given any updates.

They were in town for the weekend, and we were on our way to Ross to buy a curtain rod. It took all I had not to blurt out our secret, but I didn't want to tell her she was going to be a grandma while sitting in the backseat of my dad's truck.

I reined in my excitement and explained that it would likely be years before we brought home a baby. The answer sufficed, and we went on with our shopping.

John and I planned to share our surprise over lunch but thought it best to tell them before the food arrived in case they were too shocked to eat. As we munched on chips and salsa, I began my spiel. "We have something we want to tell you."

I'm sure my parents were waiting for the bomb to drop. There we were, eating Mexican food, just like we had the night we told them we wanted to adopt a baby from Africa. When my mom looked at me, I whispered a silent prayer before continuing.

"It looks like you're going to have a grandbaby in December. And no, I'm not pregnant," I blurted.

"But you just said it would be years before you brought a baby home from Africa," my mom said, looking confused.

"This baby isn't from Africa. There's an eighteen-year-old living at the mission who is due in December, and she wants us to adopt her baby."

Surprise spread across my parents' faces, and John and I filled them in on the details. Their excitement was obvious by all the questions they asked.

"It's meant to be," my mom said. "This just fell in your lap."

The mood was much lighter when we left the restaurant that afternoon than it had been the previous year.

My mom continued asking questions as we drove to Target to buy a crib mattress. We spent the rest of the day putting bedding in the crib and hanging curtains in the nursery. For the first time since announcing our plans to adopt, my parents genuinely seemed excited to become grandparents. We hoped John's family would feel the same way.

John's mom had voiced her concern when we bought a crib and began working on the nursery.

"I just don't want Jennifer to get her hopes up," she told John over the phone one day. After he hung up, he said, "I wanted to tell her there was going to be a baby sooner than she thought, but I wanted to wait and tell her in person."

A few weeks later, we handed John's parents a Christmas stocking. Tucked inside was a onesie that said "Born in 2011." John's mom unfolded the tiny outfit, read the words, and exclaimed, "We can finally have a baby shower!"

Our families' excitement was what I had longed for from the start. I imagined their reaction would have been similar had I told them I was expecting. International adoption was difficult for them to grasp. I was sad they weren't as eager for an African child to become part of our family. It was a foreign concept to them. But something about Allison's story made them feel connected. Maybe it was because I had a relationship with her. Maybe it was because a baby was guaranteed in December. Maybe it was because Allison's child would blend in with our family.

John's mom quickly shared the news with her friends. She strung yarn through the onesie and proudly wore it as a necklace during bunco. "God has to be all over this," her friend Debbie exclaimed. "He will work out all the details."

My mom was quick to share the news too. She definitely didn't rush to share details of our Ethiopia adoption. In fact, she didn't talk about it at all. So I was surprised when my aunt called.

"I just got off the phone with your mom," she said. "She was pretty excited to tell me she's going to be a grandmother."

My mom called almost every day, wanting to know the latest. "Did you talk to the girl today?"

"Mom, she lives where I work. I talk to her every day."

"Well, there's a couple that eats breakfast with us at Whataburger on Saturday mornings, and they adopted three children. That was fifty years ago. They were so excited when we told them about the baby."

I fought back tears and shared our concern about the birth father. "The attorney hasn't been able to find him, and we're afraid his absence in the adoption process could cause more harm than good."

"Jennifer, this is meant to be," my mom said.

I hung up the phone and burst into tears.

"What's wrong?" John asked.

"What if we don't end up with the baby? We won't be the only ones heartbroken. Our families are so excited about this. They'll be crushed if it doesn't happen."

John wrapped his arms around me and tried to reassure me. "If for some reason it doesn't work out, we will all get through it," he said.

But I wasn't so sure. I had already fallen in love with the baby and spent countless hours dreaming of our soon-to-be family of three. Our families were quickly becoming attached too.

John and I stood in an embrace in the middle of the kitchen as I continued to cry.

CHAPTER 10

Pink or Blue?

For you created my inmost being; you knit me together in my mother's womb. I praise you because I am fearfully and wonderfully made; your works are wonderful, I know that full well. My frame was not hidden from you when I was made in the secret place, when I was woven together in the depths of the earth. Your eyes saw my unformed body; all the days ordained for me were written in your book before one of them came to be.

—PSALM 139:13–16

We were less than twenty-four hours away from knowing if we would have a son or a daughter. Would I need to buy bows or baseballs? I was ready to find out, but I lacked excitement. I sat in the red oversized chair in our living room and scribbled in my journal.

The past week or two, I've had my guard up. There's so much uncertainty about the birth father. I'm scared. I know when I see the baby during the sonogram tomorrow and hear its heartbeat, I'll become even more invested in this little life. There will be ten tiny fingers and ten tiny toes, but what if we don't get to spend the rest of our lives kissing them? That's the grave reality of our situation. Until the baby is born and both parents have terminated their rights, this adoption isn't a sure thing.

It's hard to explain loving a baby that you've never seen, held, carried in your womb, or felt kick inside you. In the weeks leading up to the sonogram, Satan launched a full-fledged spiritual attack on our faith, adoption, and marriage.

In his book *Adopted for Life: The Priority of Adoption for Christian Families & Churches*, Russell D. Moore wrote,

> Adoption, as I've mentioned, is spiritual warfare in the heavenly places. Adoption is more than charity. It's spiritual warfare. What better way is there to bring the good news of Christ than to see his unwanted little brothers and sisters placed in families where they'll be raised in the nurture and admonition of the Lord?[1]

The apostle Peter knew the Devil would tempt believers, so he encouraged them to "Be self-controlled and alert. Your enemy the devil prowls around like a roaring lion looking for someone to devour. Resist him, standing firm in faith" (1 Peter 5:8). John and I faced a spiritual battle, and our only hope was to cling to God's promises.

> Finally be strong in the Lord and in His mighty power. Put on the full armor of God so you can

take your stand against the devil's schemes. For our struggle is not against flesh and blood, but against rulers, against authorities, against the powers of the dark world and against the spiritual forces of evil in the heavenly realms. Therefore put on the full armor of God, so that when the day of evil comes, you may be able to stand your guard, and after you have done everything, to stand. (Ephesians 6:10–13)

I closed my journal and allowed myself to imagine just how incredible the following day would be when we heard the words we had waited so long to hear. It's a ...

"You know I'm probably going to cry when we find out the sex of the baby," I said.

"I kind of figured you would," Allison said as we drove to her appointment.

We arrived at the doctor's office a few minutes early and found a seat. I was a bundle of nerves. I had promised John and our families that I would call the moment we received the news. There was no way I could keep the secret long enough to plan a gender-reveal party!

My phone buzzed. I looked down to see a text message from John. "I have butterflies," he wrote. "I'm ready to know." I smiled. I had butterflies too. I couldn't help but wonder if I'd be shopping for pink or blue.

Friends constantly asked if I wanted a boy or a girl. I had no preference. I knew I would be excited no matter the gender. I had waited such a long time for this moment.

"The baby just kicked," Allison said. "Do you want to feel?"

I nodded. She took my hand and placed it on her belly. "The baby doesn't move much during the day," she said. "But it's a wiggle worm at night. Sometimes it keeps me awake."

I sat with my hand on her round belly and watched it move with each kick.

"Did I tell you the baby likes music?" she asked. "I put headphones on my stomach and crank up K-LOVE, and it squirms like crazy."

I laughed at the thought of Allison with headphones on her belly. I liked knowing she let the baby listen to Christian music and that it responded.

About that time, the nurse called us back. I shot a quick text to John. "Heading back now."

Allison got situated on the exam table, and I took her hand in mine. The nurse squirted a big glob of warm jelly on her belly and began to maneuver the wand. Within seconds, we were staring at the baby's features on the huge flat-screen TV in front of us. I wiped away tears as the nurse pointed out ten tiny fingers and ten tiny toes.

"You're already crying," Allison said with a laugh. "She hasn't even told us if it's a boy or a girl."

Then I heard the words I had been waiting to hear since July.

"It's a boy," the nurse said. "And he's definitely not shy!"

I squealed with delight and squeezed Allison's hand a little too tight. I was going to have a son. "He's perfect! I have to call John." Without letting go of Allison's hand I pushed John's number on speed dial. He picked up on the first ring. "It's a boy!"

John was ecstatic. "I have a son!"

The nurse continued moving the wand across Allison's belly. He was stubborn. He didn't mind showing us he was a boy, but he didn't want us to see his face. A bit of peach fuzz covered his head, and he weighed a whopping two pounds, two ounces. The doctor said he was healthy and on track for a December 9 due date.

I looked down at Allison's hand in mine and wondered what was going through her mind. It was the first time she had seen the baby although she had carried him for six months. Did seeing his tiny features make her question her decision to place him for adoption? Was there any part of her that wanted to try and raise him on her own?

"Can we get two sets of sonogram photos?" I asked the nurse.

"She's adopting the baby," Allison said. "But I'd like to have a few photos, too, if it's okay."

The nurse handed photos to each of us—a picture of his profile, his tiny hand, and one that revealed he was definitely a boy.

As we got into the elevator to head back to the mission, I wanted to make sure Allison was okay. "How are you feeling after seeing the baby?"

"I'm fine," she said.

"It would be completely normal if you felt more attached to the baby now that you've seen his face. Now that you know it's a boy. I'd even understand if you were having second thoughts about the adoption."

"I'm not," she said. "I've made my decision. This baby is yours and John's."

"Okay," I whispered. "Do you like the name Jackson?"

The grief set in one month shy of our son's birth. Despite Allison's certainty, I knew there would come a time when the reality of her choice would catch up with her. It might not happen at the hospital or even the following week, but at some point, she would grieve the loss of the child she had carried for nine months. Grief is part of adoption. Not just for the birth family, but for the adoptive family too.

Domestic adoption had scared John and me early on. We were intimidated by the idea of an open adoption. God erased all our fears and showed us that we had an opportunity not only to make a difference in the life of a baby boy but also to love, encourage, and invest in the life of his birth mother.

In my eyes, Allison was brave, selfless, and courageous. I'm not sure I would have had the strength to carry a child for nine months, give birth, and place it in the arms of another woman. I admired Allison's choice to choose life for her child.

The afternoon after my baby shower, Allison called to say she had bought Jackson a gift. "I wanted to make sure he had something to keep him warm when he goes home from the hospital," she said. "I wasn't sure how to sign the card, so I just wrote, 'Love, Allison.'"

It was easy to get wrapped up in my own excitement and forget the pain and loss Allison was experiencing. "You can sign the card however you want," I said.

"I don't want to offend you since you're Jackson's mom."

"Jackson has two moms," I said, wiping tears from my eyes.

It was almost midnight, and I had tossed and turned for an hour. My stomach was in knots, and my mind raced. Would the phone ring tonight? Would we jump out of bed and head to the hospital?

Sleep eluded me. Every time I closed my eyes, a thousand questions ran through my mind.

When will we get the call? I'm probably going to cry when

we get word to head to the hospital. Will Jackson have hair? Will he come before or after his due date? Will Allison be okay? Do I have everything I need in the diaper bag?

I got out of bed, went into the nursery, and sat in the chair where I would soon rock my son. I looked down at my phone. Was the ringer on? I checked it for the hundredth time to make sure it wasn't turned to vibrate.

Will newborn clothes fit him? I decided to throw a few outfits the next size up into the diaper bag. I was a nervous wreck, and I wasn't even the one about to give birth. How could John be sleeping like a rock?

We needed to buy a Pack and Play, especially if we planned to go to Texas for Christmas. I hoped Story, our dog, would be okay while we were at the hospital. Her blissful doggy world was about to be rocked.

Why wasn't I sleeping? We were about to bring home a newborn, and we'd never sleep again.

I forced myself to go back to bed and try to get some sleep, all the while hoping my phone would ring.

December 9 came and went, and we still didn't have a baby. An induction was scheduled for December 14, but Allison would check into the hospital the night before.

"When do you want us to come?" I asked.

"When I check in," she said.

I called my mom to let her know the plan. A few weeks prior, she and my dad had insisted on being at the hospital. Because of the unique circumstances, John and I hadn't asked our parents to come to the hospital, but I was relieved my parents would be there.

"We would be there if you were having the baby," my mom said. "We're not coming to meet the birth mother; we are coming to support you and John."

I made it through my last day of work before taking six weeks of maternity leave. It was surreal leaving the mission, knowing my life was about to drastically change.

The morning before we left for the hospital, it dawned on me that I would be holding my son the very next day. The dog still needed a bath before I could drop her off at my friend's house, and my bag remained unpacked on my bedroom floor. But instead of taking care of the last-minute details, I found myself sitting at the kitchen table, listening to Christmas music and sobbing uncontrollably.

"Christ is the Lord, oh praise his name forever ..."

The months leading up to that moment had been a whirlwind—between my mom's cancer diagnosis and surgery, holidays at the mission, my sister's wedding, and preparing for Jackson, I had barely had a chance to let everything sink in. That morning, I allowed myself to feel every emotion—the excitement, the nerves, and the sadness.

I was humbled at all God had done. The Christmas music playing over the kitchen radio was a reminder of the miracle we were about to receive. I couldn't help but think of Mary, the mother of Jesus, and what she must have felt that very first Christmas.

> But the angel said to them, "Do not be afraid. I bring you good news of great joy that will be for all people. Today in the town of David a Savior has been born to you; he is Christ the Lord. This will be a sign to you: You will find a baby wrapped in cloths and lying in a manger."

Suddenly, a great company of the heavenly host appeared with the angel, praising God and saying, Glory to God in the highest, and on earth peace to men on whom his favor rests. When the angels had left them and gone into heaven, the shepherds said to one another, "Let's go to Bethlehem and see this thing that has happened, which the Lord has told us about." So they hurried off and found Mary and Joseph, and the baby, who was lying in the manger. When they had seen him, they spread the word concerning what had been told them about this child, and all who heard it were amazed at what the shepherds said to them. But Mary treasured up all these things and pondered them in her heart. (Luke 2:10–19)

Jackson was our Christmas miracle. I prayed his birth would reflect the true meaning of Christmas. It was all about a baby. A baby boy born in a manger in Bethlehem who changed the world.

CHAPTER 11

Then There Were Three

I prayed for this child, and the LORD has granted
me what I asked of him.
— I SAMUEL 1:27

I stared at the ceiling. It was impossible to get comfortable on the narrow vinyl couch adjacent to Allison's hospital bed. The room was silent except for the occasional beep of hospital monitors and the strong, steady beat of my son's heart. *Thump, thump, thump, thump ...*

My Little Man was a wiggle worm and giving the nurses a run for their money. Every few minutes, they had to reposition the heart monitor. He was persistent and strong-willed, even in the womb.

I wondered if Allison was asleep. She was quiet, but I had a feeling she was watching the minutes slowly tick by on the clock over the TV. She had started chattering a mile a minute the moment we checked into the hospital and hadn't stopped until around midnight, when I finally convinced her to turn off the lights and try to get some rest. "I know you're nervous," I said. "But tomorrow is going to be a long day."

I lay in the dark, silently praying and begging God for everything to go as planned. I didn't know how I could listen to that tiny heartbeat all night and not become that baby boy's mommy. Allison had said she would miss being pregnant. Did that mean she was having second thoughts about placing the baby for adoption? What if she decided to keep him? What if John and I left the hospital without him?

The nurse had pulled me aside as Allison was getting settled into her hospital room. She needed to know what the game plan was for the delivery room. Who would be in the delivery room with Allison? Who would hold the baby first? Who would cut the umbilical cord?

I sat down beside Allison and asked her how she wanted the delivery to go.

"I want you to be in the room and to hold the baby first," she said. "You can cut his umbilical cord, and then I would like to hold him for a minute."

My heart stopped. Up until that point, she had shown no interest in holding the baby. I forced a smile to hide the worry that was beginning to show on my face and was definitely creeping into my heart. "Okay, I'll let the nurses know," I said.

I shuffled to get comfortable on my makeshift bed. I didn't want to wake Allison, who was finally sleeping peacefully; her breathing was quiet and steady. But I was going to throw up. I was on the verge of tears, but I had to hold it together. Allison was already anxious. I was acting selfish in light of what she faced the following day.

I really wanted to talk to John, but I didn't want to leave Allison. He was in a room down the hall, trying to get some sleep himself. One of us needed to sleep. He later told me that he had also spent the majority of the night pleading with God.

Neither of us knew how we'd recover from the heartache if we had to leave the hospital without our son.

I drifted in and out of sleep, waking to the sound of the baby's heartbeat every hour.

At 6:00 a.m., the doctor induced. The nurse warned us we were in for a long day, that it would probably be late afternoon or early evening before the baby was born.

John sat with Allison while I took a shower in our hospital room. As I stepped into the hallway, the emotion I had bottled up the previous night worked its way to the surface. I had barely stepped into our room when the floodgates opened. I couldn't breathe and couldn't stop crying. The knot in my stomach wouldn't go away. I wanted my parents and sister to get there. I wasn't prepared to walk away from this baby if Allison changed her mind. How could I already love him so much? I was a mess and needed to pull myself together. I had to stay strong for Allison.

I stood in the shower and let the hot water wash away every fear and doubt. I cried until I couldn't shed another tear, and I prayed. I would focus on what I believed in my heart to be true: God had woven the lives of three unlikely people together because a baby boy needed a family. In the deepest crevices of my heart, I believed Allison would stick by her decision because she knew it was the best choice for her child.

I looked at my reflection in the mirror. I was about to be a mother.

I took a deep breath and walked back to Allison's room. My fear had been replaced with excitement. God had given me His peace—a peace that surpasses all understanding (Philippians 4:7).

The nurses were right. It was going to be a long day. Allison progressed very slowly. We watched each contraction on the monitor and did our best to keep her mind off the pain.

"How much do you think the baby will weigh?" I asked.

"I think he'll be seven pounds eight ounces," Allison said.

Friends asked for updates throughout the day and let us know they were praying. Justin was keeping everyone at the mission updated. The nurse encouraged John and me to go to lunch, assuring us the baby would stay put.

About the time we finished our pizza, my parents and sister arrived at the hospital. I had never been happier to see them and was glad they had been so adamant about being at the hospital.

Every few hours, the doctor checked to see if Allison had progressed. We paced up and down the hall and were discouraged when she came out each time shaking her head no. "She's only dilated to a four," she said. And a few hours later, "She's only a five."

Around 3:00 p.m., my parents left to check into their hotel, and I sent John to Sonic to get me a Dr. Pepper. My sister, who's a nurse and had worked the previous two nights, was trying to take a nap in our room.

Allison had finally been given an epidural and wasn't feeling any pain. The doctor came in to see if we were any closer to having a baby, so I stepped outside the room. The last time she had checked, Allison was only dilated to six. I assumed we still had a couple of hours before she would be ready to deliver.

"It's time to push," the doctor said.

"What? It can't be! Everyone's left the hospital!"

I raced down the hall and burst through the door of our hospital room. "Myka, Myka," I whispered. I didn't want to startle her if she was asleep. "It's time. It's time!"

My sister fumbled for her phone. She called my parents, and they rushed back to the hospital without checking into their hotel.

I called John. "You have to get back here now," I said. "She's about to push!" As I hurried to Allison's room, I sent a quick message to Justin. "She's about to push. This is really happening. I think I'm going to cry."

"I think I might too," he replied.

I silently prayed I wouldn't pass out. I'm squeamish when it comes to blood and was nervous about witnessing a birth. I also worried I would pass out when I cut the umbilical cord.

John came running down the hall and handed me the Dr. Pepper, and I went into the delivery room. John joined my parents and sister outside the hospital room door and waited.

I took my spot beside Allison and got my camera ready.

"Okay," the doctor said. "It's time to push."

I squeezed Allison's shoulder. "You can do this," I said. "You're doing great."

Four pushes later, at 4:02 p.m., the doctor held up the biggest baby I had ever seen. "I think we might have guessed wrong on his weight," I said. "I don't think his newborn clothes are going to fit."

Allison laughed, and I choked back tears.

His head was covered in dark brown hair, and he had the fullest lips and the chubbiest cheeks. Within moments of his first breath, he began to cry. The sound drifted to the hallway where John and my family waited anxiously. They said it was the most wonderful sound they had ever heard.

"Who's cutting the umbilical cord?" the doctor asked.

I squeezed Allison's shoulder. "You were a rock star," I said. I left her side to join the nurses who were busy cleaning up my son.

The nurse took my camera and handed me the scissors. I prayed I wouldn't pass out. After I cut the cord, the nurses began weighing, measuring, and getting the baby's footprints. I took his tiny hand in mine, and he wrapped it around my finger.

"He's eight pounds thirteen ounces," the nurse said.

"Did you hear that, Allison? We were way off," I said.

The nurse swaddled him and placed my son in my arms for the first time. I was oblivious to the hustle and bustle going on around me as I gazed at him. Tears streamed down my face as I walked to the door and introduced Jackson Henry to his daddy, his Pop and Lolli, and his Auntie M. There wasn't a dry eye. He was only a few minutes old, and we were already gaga over him.

I will never forget the look on my family members' faces. Every doubt they might have had was quickly replaced with love, wonder, and amazement. We had witnessed a miracle.

After a few family photos, I took Jackson and placed him in the arms of the woman who had chosen to give him life. I glanced at Allison and then down at my son. He had her lips.

She held him for a few moments but didn't say much. The nurse took photos of the three of us—photos I will cherish for the rest of my life. Photos I'll show Jackson when I tell him the amazing story God wrote for our family.

"Don't give your parents too much trouble," Allison said. "It's time to go back to your mom." As she handed Jackson back to me, she said, "I hope the next time I have a baby, I can take care of it."

"I hope so too," I said, cradling Jackson in my arms as I wiped away tears.

I rolled Jackson to our hospital room, and from that moment on, he was in our care. John and I were completely smitten and passed him around like a sack of potatoes. We gave him his first bath, which he hated, and spent most of the night letting Jackson sleep in our arms. We had waited so long for that moment.

For months, I had tried to play the birth out in my mind. At times, I wanted to get the surprise phone call in the middle of the night, grab our bags, and rush to the hospital. I'm glad God had other plans. Had it happened that way, we probably would have missed Jackson's birth, and my family wouldn't have stood outside the hospital room and heard Jackson's first cries.

Nothing I imagined about the day my son was born could compare to how it actually went. From the moment we checked into the hospital, the nurses and staff treated Allison with the utmost respect. They were sensitive to the fact that she had chosen adoption for her child, but they also celebrated and shared in John's and my joy.

The following morning, the nurse who took care of Allison the first night and who had repositioned Jackson's heart monitor a thousand times, stopped by to meet our Little Man. When I handed Jackson to her, she oohed and aahed over his beautiful lips and dark hair. "I'm really glad I got to be your nurse," she said. "I could relate to what you all were going through. I was adopted and ran away from home when I was fifteen years old. I got pregnant and had every intention of giving the baby up for adoption. But when I held him, I just couldn't let him go."

I couldn't believe God had allowed such an amazing woman and nurse to be a part of our story.

"I understand what your birth mom is going through and all the emotions involved. I've experienced all of them." She handed Jackson back to me. "He's beautiful, and he's lucky to have parents who love him so much."

"Thank you," I said. "God knew we would need a nurse who truly understood the joy and grief of adoption."

Her story wasn't the only one that touched our hearts during our forty-eight-hour hospital stay. Allison had been attending church, and the pastor and his wife were at the hospital when

Jackson was born. The pastor's wife shared with my mom that she was adopted. "Seeing your joy when you first saw your grandson gave me a glimpse of what it must have been like for my family when they adopted me," she said.

<hr/>

We wrapped Jackson in the OU blanket Allison had given him and walked next door to her room. She had asked to see him one last time before she left the hospital. "I heard him cry a few times last night," she said as we walked into the room.

I couldn't imagine being in her shoes—just giving birth, handing over her child, and then having to listen to him cry during the night. The least the hospital could have done was put her in a room a few doors down from ours. "Would you like to hold him?" I asked.

She nodded, and I handed Jackson to her. I wasn't nervous or afraid. I wanted to capture the moment in my memory so I could share it with Jackson one day.

Just like the first time she held him, her words were few. After a few moments, she handed him back to me. She never cried (at least that I saw). She hugged me, picked up her bag, and walked out of the room.

I held Jackson and cried. God had answered my prayer for a son. I guess He had answered Allison's prayer too.

We went back to our room and placed Jackson in his car seat. We covered him with the OU blanket and waited to be discharged. Shortly after, we left the hospital a family of three. Our Missing Linck was finally home.

CHAPTER 12

Bringing Home the Missing Linck

He tends his flock like a shepherd: He gathers the lambs in his arms and carries them close to his heart; he gently leads those that have young.
—ISAIAH 40:11

When my friends were dishing out advice at my baby shower, no one told me I'd lock myself in the bathroom and cry hysterically just weeks after Jackson's birth. No one prepared me for the crazy thoughts and emotions that resulted from sleep deprivation. I contemplated divorce. I wanted to get in my car and drive away. I didn't recognize the person I saw in the mirror.

"I'm never adopting a newborn again!" I yelled one night as Jackson screamed.

Our social worker had asked what we dreaded most about bringing home a newborn. I didn't have to think twice. The answer was easy. "I won't be able to sleep when I want to," I said.

The first weeks of motherhood (who am I kidding? the first *months*) nearly sent me over the edge. My mom's words constantly came to mind. "Jennifer, raising a child will be the hardest thing you ever do." She was right.

Jackson was only one week old when the colic-induced screams began. Every muscle in my body tensed up. I knew I needed to relax before Jackson sensed my tension and became more upset. I rocked him. I bounced him. Nothing worked. Desperation began setting in.

"Let me try," John said. He took Jackson and swaddled him as tight as he could. He rubbed his back. He walked around the house, bouncing him. But Jackson's screams pierced the night air. John was more anxious than me when he handed Jackson back.

I was out of ideas and distressed. I put Jackson in his car seat and lay on the nursery floor, barely able to keep my eyes open, and rocked the car seat. He screamed, and I cried.

Around midnight, John had a suggestion. "Let's go for a drive. He always sleeps in the car."

It was worth a shot. Nothing else was working. We loaded Jackson in the car and drove all over Oklahoma City. The vibration of the car soothed him, and within moments, he was asleep.

So began three long months of sleepless, scream-filled nights. We tried everything. We switched his formula more than once, we rubbed his tummy and moved his legs, and we put his car seat on the dryer. Gas drops and gripe water didn't even bring him relief. The only thing that seemed to alleviate his pain was long car rides. We put a lot of miles on our car for the sake of our sanity.

Jackson slept in our arms or in the car seat the first three months of his life. When he dozed off, we'd tiptoe to our room, slide into bed, and pray he'd sleep if only for an hour. No such luck. Within minutes, he'd wake up, screaming.

The nights I feared I was near my breaking point, I would hold him tight and sing softly, "Jesus loves me this I know, for the Bible tells me so ..." The words seemed to calm him and me. Old hymns, some I hadn't sung in years, began flooding my mind. Every night I sang. Every night I asked Jesus to make the crying stop. There were many nights that I sang through tears of frustration. I didn't know how I would make it through another night.

When I felt desperate, I clung to God's promises. During those long nights, I often found myself repeating Colossians 11:1: "Being strengthened with all power according to His glorious might so that I might have great endurance and patience." I was weary, but I wanted to endure, and I definitely needed more patience. I also held onto the promises found in Isaiah 40:11 and Psalm 139:10, respectively, "He gently leads those that have young" and "God's hand will guide me."

It didn't take long for me to realize I needed Jesus more than ever before. It was impossible to be the mother God wanted me to be in my own strength. I failed daily. I got discouraged and wanted to quit. God reminded me that His strength was made perfect in my weakness. "But he said to me, 'My grace is sufficient for you, for my power is made perfect in weakness.' Therefore I will boast all the more gladly about my weaknesses, so that Christ's power may rest on me" (2 Corinthians 12:9). He promised to cover me with His mercy and grace, which I needed in order to face each new day.

The nurse at the hospital had warned me about postpartum depression. "Just because you didn't give birth doesn't mean you won't experience some baby blues," she said.

Guilt, shame, and depression hovered over me like storm clouds. Jackson's colic wasn't getting any better, and soon the screaming became an around-the-clock occurrence. I was about to pull my hair out. There had to be something we could do.

I made an appointment with our pediatrician and was thankful when Jackson screamed through the entire appointment. At least she got a glimpse of what we were dealing with. "I think this is colic and a severe case of acid reflux," the doctor said.

There wasn't much we could do for the colic, but she prescribed medicine for the acid reflux. Within a few weeks, Jackson began feeling better. The days were peaceful, but we still dreaded the nights.

I'll never forget taking Jackson to get his pictures made for Valentine's Day. Casey, the photographer, had taken our wedding photos, photos of John and me before Jackson was born, and Jackson's newborn photos. I was so excited to have his picture made, but it was obvious right from the start that Jackson wasn't going to cooperate. He wailed. The situation began to spin out of control. I grew frustrated. I just wanted a few photos. Why was he always crying?

Casey took Jackson and began to bounce him. "Girl, I've been there," she said. "My son was so colicky. You need to go and buy Nutramagin. Don't wait another day. It's the only thing that works. Believe me, we tried everything."

I was hesitant to switch Jackson's formula again, but I was willing to take a chance if it worked.

I went to the store, spent the thirty-five dollars for a can that probably wouldn't get us through a week, and prayed it would be our saving grace.

It wasn't long before we noticed the formula was working. Jackson was still fussy, but there was a dramatic difference in our nights. John and I deemed Nutramagin "liquid gold." Our bank account took a big blow, but we gained sleep and sanity.

<center>~~~</center>

John and I were struggling. Our families lived out of state, and the only support we had were our friends Justin and Jessica. I lost count how many nights they came over and sat through the crying so we wouldn't have a nervous breakdown.

We stopped going to church. Not because we wanted to but because the few times we went, Jackson either had explosive poop diapers or screamed the entire time. Nobody noticed our absence. Nobody called to check on us. It was a lonely and difficult time.

My only outlet was my blog. I wrote about the colic, the crazy thoughts running through my mind, and the difficulty I was having adjusting to motherhood.

"You need to watch what you're telling people," my mom said one day on the phone. "What will they think? You prayed for this baby, and now you're complaining."

I could feel the anger rising in me. I wanted to hang up on her. I was falling apart, and she was criticizing me. "I'm not going to slap a smile on my face and pretend everything is okay," I said. "This is hard, and someone needs to talk about it." I had been open and honest about my infertility. I had shared the joys and heartaches of adoption. So I was determined to be honest post-adoption, even if it made others uncomfortable.

According to an article in *Adoptive Families* magazine, "Post-Adoption Depression Syndrome may affect one in every ten new adoptive mothers and as many as 65 percent of adoptive parents experience some depression after adopting their children."[1]

Guilt consumed me. I felt like I was failing as a mother. I missed my job. I couldn't keep my house clean, and I just wanted to sleep. I felt guilty for feeling guilty.

Hopelessness plagued me. I wondered if the colic would ever get better or if Jackson would ever sleep in his crib. Several people said we just had to make it to the twelve-week mark, and we'd be amazed how much easier things would become. I was counting the days.

The stress began taking a toll on our marriage. John and I were exhausted. We never went to bed at the same time because one of us always held Jackson so he'd sleep. Our only conversations that didn't revolve around the baby happened on our midnight drives.

John had little experience in the baby department. Before becoming parents, he refused to hold babies until they were several months old. So his anxiety was off the charts. He doubted his ability to care for Jackson, and the crying just added to his apprehension. I couldn't leave the house without getting a frantic phone call. I felt like a single parent and began resenting John.

"You need to man up!" I told him one night as I took Jackson from him.

He was frazzled, and I was mad. We'd been doing the same song and dance for months, and I had had enough of his inadequacies. "Sometimes I think it would be easier to do this by myself."

The look on his face was proof my words had stung. "Fine, why don't you just leave?" he yelled.

"I'm sure you'd like that. It would make things a lot easier for you."

I looked at my husband and saw a stranger. How had things deteriorated so quickly? Divorce had never crossed my mind, but that night the Devil made it seem like an easy way out. We had to do something before the situation spun further out of control and we wound up sitting in an attorney's office.

I tried telling John how unhappy I was on more than one occasion, but I could never adequately express how I felt, and I didn't want to hurt his feelings. He didn't think our marriage was in shambles, but I felt our problems ran deeper than sleep deprivation and nonexistent date nights. I was going through an identity crisis. I didn't know who I was aside from being Jackson's mom.

"I made an appointment with a counselor," I said one night when John got home from work.

"Do you want me to go with you?"

"I think I'd like to start by going alone, if that's okay."

I had seen a counselor twice after the doctor told me I was infertile. I stopped going because I was terrified our agency would reject our request to adopt if they knew about the sessions. We knew of couples who had been denied by agencies because one or both had used antidepressants or had attended counseling. But after two visits, the counselor didn't think it was necessary for me to continue with the sessions anyway. "You're dealing with the grief of not being able to conceive," she said. "You aren't in a state of crisis." So I stopped going. Now I sat on the couch opposite my new counselor during our first session and wondered why I had waited so long to make the appointment.

When our hour was up, she ran down the list of loss and pain I had experienced in such a short period of time: the inability to have children, the side effects of PCOS, my loved ones' inability to understand and support our decision to adopt, bringing home a newborn with colic, leaving a job I loved, the strain on my marriage, and trying to figure out who I was aside from Jackson's mommy. I had never stopped to consider how much loss was associated with our story. I hadn't allowed myself to fully grieve.

The current stress I was under was bringing all the old hurts to the surface. Unless I dealt with the pain, my marriage would continue to suffer.

I prayed and continued seeing my counselor, and John and I began having honest and sometimes difficult conversations. We both had to work through issues we didn't even realize we had. Becoming parents quickly revealed how selfish we truly were.

It has taken a lot of time. We've both had to forgive, and we've had to make our relationship a priority. We're far from perfect, but our marriage is growing stronger each day. We survived those turbulent months, and we slowly started to like each other again.

When John and I were dating, he wanted me to return to work after having children, but I wanted to be a stay-at-home mom. We were barely home from the hospital when John began playing with our budget to see if we could survive on one income. He wanted me to be the stay-at-home mom I had dreamed of being. But I wrestled with the decision to go back to work.

After six weeks of maternity leave, I tried working part-time, but I knew I was supposed to stay home and be the mother I had prayed to become for so long. Leaving my job at the mission took a huge leap of faith. In fact, quitting was harder than obeying God when He called us to adopt. It wasn't that I disliked being home with Jackson. I loved taking him to story time and having lazy pajama days. But I loved my job because it gave me a sense of purpose, and I really didn't want to give up my paycheck.

Pride kept me from giving my notice sooner than I did. I had worked since I was eighteen years old, and the thought of relying on John to provide wasn't exactly appealing. My independent side rebelled. I didn't like the idea of having to ask for money or having to explain my purchases to John. Only one thing caused heated debates between John and me, and that was our bank balance.

As I struggled to walk away from my paycheck, something Jen Hatmaker wrote convinced me. "God was confronting me with my greed, excess materialism, consumerism, envy, pride, and comfort ..."[2] I loved my job, but I was staying for the wrong reasons. I would miss working where Jesus Christ was priority. My coworkers had become friends, and I would miss the clients who hugged me each morning and asked about Jackson. Through the joy and the sadness I experienced during my time at the mission, God had changed me. He taught me to love and accept those the world so often deems unworthy. Children had climbed in and out of my lap, filling my empty heart as I waited to become a mother. I had tied their shoes, shared my breakfast, and tried to love them the way Jesus wanted me to.

Leaving was bittersweet. As I drove home on my last day, I cried. I left the mission, but the mission would always have a piece of my heart. It was where God had fulfilled His promise to me.

Butterflies fluttered in my stomach. We had waited six months to finalize Jackson's adoption, and April 30, 2012, would officially be his Gotcha Day!

Allison had appeared before the judge a few weeks after Jackson's birth. John and I had sat in the back row of the courtroom and watched as the judge asked her if she was certain of her decision to relinquish her rights. He had been gruff, making sure she realized how serious her decision was and that it couldn't be changed. My mom reassured me that the mood of the courtroom would be much brighter than it had been the day Allison had appeared. The judge had intimidated me, and I worried he'd be just as serious when we stood before him.

"I really want a photo with the judge for Jackson's adoption book," I told John as we drove to the courthouse. "What if he doesn't want to take a photo with us?" I didn't know why I was so nervous. From the moment Jackson was born, he had been mine. I didn't need a judge to tell me I was his mother.

Our attorney was waiting for us when we arrived at the courthouse, as were Justin and Jessica. As we walked into the courtroom, I was prepared for another serious hearing. However, my mom was right again.

"Feel free to walk around the courtroom and take as many photos as you'd like," the court clerk said.

I handed my camera to Jessica as John, Jackson, and I approached the bench. After we were sworn in, our attorney began the proceeding.

"Your Honor, on behalf of John and Jennifer Linck, I would like to request that the adoption of their son be finalized. He has been in their custody since his birth on December 14."

"Are you sure you're ready for all the ups and downs of parenthood?" the judge asked.

"Yes, sir," I said enthusiastically.

"No, you're not," the judge said with a smile. "He's going to stay out late, and you'll worry yourself sick. It's going to get harder."

I couldn't imagine anything being as hard as the first few months had been. We all laughed at the judge's sense of humor. There were no tears that day. Just hearts full of gratitude.

"I hereby declare the adoption of Jackson Henry Linck final," the judge said as he whacked his gavel on the bench.

"Your Honor, would it be okay if we took a photo with you?" I asked.

"Of course," he said. "Why don't we stand in front of the bench?" He stepped down, and we gathered around for the photo.

"One, two, three," Jessica said. The flash went off, capturing the moment we officially became a Forever Family.

I peeked in on Jackson and found him wide awake. He wasn't hungry, and he wasn't crying. He just wasn't sleepy. I probably should have left him alone, but there would be a day when my Little Man wouldn't want to be rocked.

I stared at the verse painted on the nursery wall like I had done so many times before. "I prayed for this child, and the LORD has granted me what I asked of Him" (1 Samuel 1:27). I rocked Jackson by the glow of the streetlight pouring into the room through the cracks in the blinds. It was after midnight, my first Mother's Day.

Our families were in town to celebrate the occasion as well as Jackson's dedication at church.

I had called Allison the previous day—Birth Mother's Day—to thank her for the precious gift she had given me. She had sent me a beautiful Mother's Day card and had signed it "Much Gratitude, Allison."

But like the night before the sonogram, I was overcome with grief. Jackson sucked on his pacifier as I rocked him. I silently prayed for my baby boy and thanked God for letting me be his mommy. The weekend would be full of joy and celebration for me, but I knew that wasn't the case for Jackson's birth mom.

I prayed for God to comfort Allison. I kissed Jackson's head and held him a little tighter. Allison would never rock him. She would never walk into his room in the early morning hours and be greeted by his crazy bed-head and wide, toothless grin.

Something about that realization made me sad. Would Allison feel sad, or would the day pass without any thought of Jackson? Would Mother's Day always bring such a mix of emotions?

I sat in the dark, holding my son as he slept, and the tears began to fall. I realized Allison would always be a part of my Mother's Day celebrations; after all, she was Jackson's mother too.

⚬≈⚬

I began sorting through a lot of junk during my counseling sessions. We discussed my infertility, the PCOS, our decision to adopt, the stress of a colicky baby, and my marriage. I got things off my chest that I had kept inside for years. Just spilling my guts did wonders for my depression.

The counselor encouraged me to see my doctor and readdress the PCOS. I still had irregular periods, and my hormones were completely out of whack. My hormone levels hadn't been checked since I had been diagnosed two years earlier, so my doctor ordered labs before deciding how to best address the PCOS.

When the test results came back, my doctor announced that my hormone levels were fine. "They're absolutely beautiful," she said. "Had you tried to get pregnant this month, it just might have happened."

"So what are you saying?" I asked. "Do I not have PCOS?"

"These levels don't reflect PCOS," she said.

I was shocked. I didn't jump up and down and thank God for healing me. Rather, something didn't add up. I didn't want to have PCOS, but when I was diagnosed, I had every symptom of the syndrome. A sonogram had clearly shown tiny cysts covering my ovaries, and my doctor had definitely said, "You have PCOS." It seemed to me she was jumping the gun a bit, retracting her previous diagnosis after one round of blood work.

"I think you're just one of those people who have an irregular cycle," my doctor said. "You may or may not ovulate, which means fertility drugs will be needed if you ever want to conceive."

"Well, I don't," I said. Counseling had helped me realize that I had never wanted to be pregnant. What I had wanted was to be a mother. Nothing about morning sickness and epidurals appealed to me. Each month that I stared at a pregnancy test, a part of me prayed for a plus sign, but only because I was desperate to be a mother. But a larger part of me was terrified of seeing a positive result and was always more relieved than I should have been when the sign didn't appear. Deep down, I did *not* want to be pregnant.

Having PCOS meant it was unlikely I would conceive without the help of fertility drugs. If I didn't have PCOS, there was a tiny chance I could conceive. There wasn't a thing about that realization that I liked.

I've had to let go of my fear of pregnancy and trust God with the outcome. It's been a constant struggle, but the more I've prayed about it and have talked to my counselor, I believe God knows my heart. Adoption is still His plan for our family. There are so many children yearning for families.

I don't want to get pregnant. I don't feel a need to have a biological child. There are a lot of people who don't understand my decision. Some people think I'm selfish and question my faith. I'm used to those people. They were the ones who constantly said, "I just know you'll get pregnant" throughout our adoption journey. It's the man who asked why I didn't want a *real* baby upon finding out we had adopted. It's the people who pushed fertility treatments and disagreed with adoption fund-raising.

Biology doesn't make someone a mother. Love does. And I love Jackson something fierce. I can't imagine loving him more, and I could never love him any less.

CHAPTER 13

Letting Go of a Dream

Forget the former things; do not dwell on the past.
See, I am doing a new thing! Now it springs up;
do you not perceive it? I am making a way in the
desert and streams in the wasteland.
—ISAIAH 43:18–19

We had been on the Ethiopian wait list for nine months when our agency reported another increase in wait times. Because of our agency's policy that children must be a year apart in age, our adoption had been placed on hold when Jackson was born. It would be at least nineteen months before we received a referral, and there were ninety families ahead of us on the list.

Two years prior, our agency had placed 150 children in families. The following year that number dropped to fifty-five, and it continued to decrease. Only twenty children had been placed that year.

The statistics were depressing, and we faced a tough decision. Did we wait it out and risk the entire program closing, or did we walk away? A major factor in our decision was the money. Each year, our paperwork expired and had to be updated, which cost money. We would likely have had to update paperwork several times before completing an adoption, and our bank account didn't have unlimited funds.

The executive director of our local adoption agency shared with us that there was a huge need for families to adopt African American and biracial children in Oklahoma. Children in our own state needed families, and of course, God had given both John and me a heart for African children. The decision was grueling, and I struggled with walking away from the program. I e-mailed a friend and Ethiopian adoptive mom and asked for her advice.

"I'll be honest. I would run and run fast," she wrote. ":(You are open to babies, and there are babies here, lots of babies. Your agency has a very long wait list and a weakening in country program." She wasn't the only one who was concerned our agency's entire program could shut down.

"I've been feeling like we should leave the program," I replied.

"Here's the deal. Where is God calling you?" she wrote. "That's the bottom line. Then you make a shirt that says 'Audience of One' like we did when things were tough, and you walk in obedience to our King, not looking to the right or to the left."

I didn't understand why God would call us to Ethiopia if we weren't going to bring children home. But during my Bible study one night, He began revealing the big picture. I had to map out periods (good and bad) in my life so I could see how God's plans had been accomplished.

I wrote a list of events in my journal, and God's plan became clear:

- Infertility and depression led to the decision to adopt.
- God led us to Ethiopia, which He used to soften my heart toward the poor and the orphan.

- I prayed a dramatic prayer for God to show me how I could serve the poor in my own community, and He opened the door for my job at the mission.
- Five months after starting the job, I met Jackson's birth mom.

Maybe God had called us to Ethiopia for no other reason than to change me and break my heart for what broke His.

It was not an easy decision to walk away from the Ethiopia program. I closed my eyes and saw the faces of so many Ethiopian orphans, and my heart ached. But I knew God was redirecting John and me to include adopting an African American or biracial child in our own state.

Leaving the Ethiopia program was hard enough, but it became even more difficult when people close to us didn't agree with our decision. We faced criticism from individuals who had helped us financially. They wanted their money back if we weren't going to proceed with our international adoption.

"Well, we've been talking. When we gave you the money for the adoption, it was intended for an African baby," one friend said. "So if you decide to leave the program, we would like our money back."

I couldn't believe what I was hearing. I felt my cheeks turn red. I was an angry mama bear, ready to defend my cub. Was she insinuating that Jackson's adoption wasn't as important as that of an African child? "I'll get a check in the mail to you," I said.

"You can keep the money until you make a decision," she said.

I knew if we kept the money I would be tempted to continue with our Ethiopian adoption, even though it was clear that God was calling us elsewhere. John and I weren't angry that we had to return the money. We just assumed that our friends' gifts were so John and I could adopt a child. We didn't realize there were stipulations attached. The thought that people viewed international adoption as more important than domestic adoption broke my heart. Every child deserves to have a family.

I questioned our decision to fund-raise, but God reminded me that He had a purpose for it. He wanted to include others in the incredible story He had written. Having to return people's money was another way God confirmed that we were to leave the Ethiopia program.

I knew I was supposed to write a book about our journey and share the story of God's faithfulness. Writing has always come easy to me, but I was resistant when I felt God nudge me to speak. I had just returned from a writing conference where I had met with potential publishers, and each one said I needed a bigger platform. They encouraged me to book speaking engagements.

I had no idea where to begin, and asking if I could speak to a group intimidated me. I kept ignoring God's still, small voice, so He decided to speak louder.

We were visiting my parents' church in Texas when something the preacher said lit a fire under me. "Jesus has done something in your life, and it's your responsibility to share it," their preacher, Werth, said.

And there it was again. That still, small voice I could no longer ignore. "Ask Werth if you can speak on Orphan Sunday."

After the service, I told Werth I'd be calling him to discuss something I felt God was asking me to do. It took a few weeks, but I finally got up the nerve. I rambled like an idiot as I explained what the publishers encouraged me to do, my dream of writing a book, and how I felt God had opened a door of opportunity the Sunday I visited his church.

"We would be honored to have you speak at church and to host Orphan Sunday," Werth said.

We spent the next few weeks preparing for the service. I would share our adoption story before the sermon. We'd also show the Orphan Sunday video and give church members the opportunity to sponsor children through Compassion International. The day our Compassion box arrived in the mail, I looked through the sponsorship packets and prayed over each child. I hoped every one of them would receive sponsors during our event.

Orphan Sunday finally arrived, and I questioned if I had heard God right. Would anyone really care about what I had to say? I felt like Moses when he came across the burning bush in Exodus 3:11-12:

> "Who am I, that I should go to Pharaoh and bring the Israelites out of Egypt?" Moses had asked.

> God answered, "I will be with you."

> Moses continued to question God. "O Lord, I have never been eloquent, neither in the past nor since you have spoken to your servant. I am slow of speech and tongue." (Exodus 4:10)

God knew Moses was capable if he depended on Him. "Now go; I will help you speak and will teach you what to say." (Exodus 4:12)

During the first service, I was crying before the video concluded. I had a hard time holding it together as I shared how

God had brought Jackson into our lives. I didn't dare look at my family. My sister later told me they all had cried and that my dad kept kissing Jackson on the head. Jackson slept through the entire thing.

I prayed that my voice would be strong and that I would keep my composure during the second service. Just like He did for Moses, God spoke through me, and I believe eyes were opened not only to the international orphan crisis but also to the children in the United States in need of Forever Families. But I was discouraged when only two children were sponsored.

"We helped two kids," John said. "Those kids now have someone praying for them and will have clean drinking water, medicine, and a chance at an education."

I knew John was right, but I felt I had failed the kids who didn't receive sponsors that day.

❦

Christmas was only a few weeks away when my mom called to say she wanted to do things differently. Instead of exchanging gifts with her side of the family on Christmas Eve, she had a better idea. "What if we all pooled our money together and sponsored one of the children you talked about at church?" she asked.

Joy filled my heart as I listened to my mom's idea. She was beginning to understand the burning desire I had to help orphans. God whispered to my heart, "Jennifer, this is happening because you were a voice for those kids in November. Even if one gets sponsored, you have made a difference."

"I think that's a great idea," I said.

My mom sent a letter to her family explaining her idea, and they loved it. So that year they chose to forgo Christmas presents to help a child in need. They put Acts 20:35 into action. "In everything I did, I showed you that by this kind of hard work we must help the weak, remembering the words the Lord Jesus himself said: 'It's more blessed to give than to receive.'"

They chose to give a child the gift of hope, a true reflection of Christmas. My family's sponsorship is now making an eternal difference in the life of a little boy in India.

———— ❧ ————

I couldn't believe the text message I had just received. A couple John and I knew was preparing to adopt again, just one year after bringing their first son home.

They are ready to bring home another child? I thought. When Jackson was born, our initial plan was to start the adoption process again when he turned one year old. But we quickly realized we weren't ready to add to our family. We had just recovered from the long, sleepless nights of colic-induced screaming and were facing a new battle—temper tantrums around 3:00 a.m. from a toddler who wanted to play instead of sleep. John and I both questioned whether we had the energy and strength to adopt a newborn again. The thought of another baby with colic made the idea of an only child enticing.

I had just returned from an adoption retreat where many families had adopted four, five, and six children. Between those big families and the news I had just received, I felt completely inadequate. "What's wrong with us that we don't think we can handle another child yet?" I asked God.

Satan was having a blast. When you compare yourself to others, you're sure to feel like crap.

The more I thought and prayed about it, God reminded me that His plan for each of us is different. Just because John and I weren't ready to adopt again didn't mean we never would be.

God could change our hearts in the blink of an eye. He'd done it before. And I have learned that His timetable is usually not the same as mine. "For my thoughts are not your thoughts, neither are your ways my ways. As the heavens are higher than the earth, so are my ways higher than your ways and my thoughts than your thoughts" (Isaiah 55:8–9).

God didn't want comparison to steal my joy. When we compare ourselves to others and what God is doing in their lives, we aren't focusing on what God wants to do in us. Comparing ourselves to others threatens our own walk with God, and we quickly forget all that God has done for us.

I was envious that God was growing the other couple's family. I wanted God to write a story like that for us. But wait … He already had. Our adoption story is one that *only* God could have written. How many people plan to adopt from Ethiopia, accept a job at the local homeless shelter, and meet the birth mother of their future son?

Comparison is a trap. The Devil wants to snare you, but God wants to free you from the comparison game. The Bible says, "Be alert and of sober mind. Your enemy the devil prowls around like a roaring lion looking for someone to devour" (1 Peter 5:8).

John and I aren't sure what the future holds. We trust God will make it very clear if and when we are to adopt again. Until then, we will continue to be a voice for orphans everywhere. We will educate others about adoption and never take for granted the greatest gift we ever received—our son.

EPILOGUE

I sat in a sea of 450 women. We were strangers, yet we shared an undeniable bond. Our hearts beat to the same rhythm.

Thump, thump. Hearts beating for adoption.

Thump, thump. Hearts beating for the orphan.

Thump, thump. Hearts beating for Jesus.

I tried to swallow the knot lodged in my throat, but it wouldn't budge. Tears trickled down my cheeks as a melody of voices proclaimed God's faithfulness.

> If faith can move the mountains
> let the mountains move
> we come with expectation
> waiting here for You ...
> With our hands lifted high in praise
> and it's You we adore
> Singing Alleluia[1]

The words fell from my lips in a whisper as the realization of what I was witnessing sank in.

Photos of children with their Forever Families flashed one after another on the screen in front of me.

Many of the families had walked through hell to bring their children home. God had placed adoption on their hearts, and because of their obedience and His faithfulness, more than a thousand children were no longer considered orphans. They were adopted. They were loved.

Each family photo reflected the heart of God. Not a single family looked the same—some were big, some were small, some included special-needs children—and many families had dared to cross racial lines. Each Forever Family was a glimpse of His creativity. Milk chocolate, toffee, cinnamon, and peach—color didn't matter. Love did.

Then it happened. I held my breath as our photo popped onto the screen for a brief second.

There we were, the family I had yearned and prayed for, standing with the judge on Jackson's Gotcha Day. I was experiencing God's miracle for our family all over again. In that moment, every sleepless night and every difficult moment from the past fifteen months faded away. I was overcome by the love of my heavenly Father. He answered the deepest cries of my heart when Jackson was placed in my arms.

I love Jackson more than words can express, but the affection I have for my son doesn't compare to God's love for me or for you, sweet reader. As Ephesians 1:4–6 says,

> He chose us in him before the creation of the world to be holy and blameless in his sight. In love, he predestined us to be adopted as his sons through Jesus Christ, in accordance with his pleasure and will—to the praise of his glorious grace, which he has freely given us in the One he loves.

God doesn't want us to remain spiritual orphans. He longs that we be adopted into His family for eternity.

John 3:16 says, "For God so loved the world that he gave his one and only Son, that whoever believes in him shall not perish but have eternal life." Have you been adopted as His son or daughter through Jesus Christ?

It has been my constant prayer that God receive every ounce of glory from the words on these pages—that the extravagant love of our Savior be proclaimed through our story and leave those who don't know Him thirsting for more. Jesus said, "Whoever drinks the water I give him will never thirst. Indeed, the water I give him will become in him a spring of water welling up to eternal life" (John 4:14).

As I type these final words and you close this book, "I pray that you, being rooted and established in love, may have power, together with all the saints, to grasp how wide and long and high and deep is the love of Christ, and to know this love surpasses knowledge—that you may be filled to the measure of all the fullness of God" (Ephesians 3:17–19).

NOTES

CHAPTER 1

1. Kelly Minter, *No Other Gods: Confronting Our Modern-Day Idols* (Nashville, LifeWay Press, 2007), 41.
2. Kelly Minter, *No Other Gods: Confronting Our Modern-Day Idols* (Nashville, LifeWay Press, 2007), 45.
3. Kelly Minter, *Ruth: Love, Loss, & Legacy* (Nashville, LifeWay Press, 2009), 109.

CHAPTER 2

1. Jack Hayford, *New Spirit-Filled Life Bible: Kingdom Equipping Through the Power of the Word* (Nashville, Thomas Nelson, 2012), 1753.
2. Kelly Minter, *No Other Gods: Confronting Our Modern-Day Idols* (Nashville, LifeWay Press, 2007), 133.

CHAPTER 3

1. FFH, *What It Feels Like* (single), 2009 by Catapult, Compact disc.
2. Kelly Minter, *No Other Gods: Confronting Our Modern-Day Idols* (Nashville, LifeWay Press, 2007), 170.

CHAPTER 4

1. David Platt, *Radical: Taking Back Your Faith From the American Dream* (Colorado Springs, Multnomah Books, 2010), 195.

2. David Platt, *Radical: Taking Back Your Faith From the American Dream* (Colorado Springs, Multnomah Books, 2010), 216.

3. Natalie Grant, *Make A Way,* Relentless, 2008 by Curb, Compact disc.

CHAPTER 6

1. Steven Furtick, *Sun Stand Still: What Happens When You Dare to Ask God for the Impossible* (Colorado Springs, Multnomah Books, 2010), 30.

2. Steven Furtick, *Sun Stand Still: What Happens When You Dare to Ask God for the Impossible* (Colorado Springs, Multnomah Books, 2010), 45.

3. Laura Story, *Blessings,* Blessings, 2011 by Columbia, Compact disc.

4. Sarah Young, *Jesus Calling: Enjoying Peace in His Presence* (Nashville, Thomas Nelson, 2004), 175.

5. Steven Furtick, *Sun Stand Still: What Happens When You Dare to Ask God for the Impossible* (Colorado Springs, Multnomah Books, 2010), 84-85.

CHAPTER 7

1. Francis Chan, *Crazy Love: Overwhelmed By A Relentless God* (Colorado Springs, David. C. Cook, 2008), 89.

2. Francis Chan, *Crazy Love: Overwhelmed By A Relentless God* (Colorado Springs, David. C. Cook, 2008), 78.

3. Kelly Minter, *No Other Gods: Confronting Our Modern-Day Idols* (Nashville, LifeWay Press, 2007), 64.

4. Kelly Minter, *No Other Gods: Confronting Our Modern-Day Idols* (Nashville, LifeWay Press, 2007), 64.

5. Heather Hendrick, "Reality is a Weighty Thing," *Sit A Spell* (blog), October 4, 2010, http://allthingshendrick. blogspot.com/2010/10/reailty-is-weighty-thing.html

6. Cedermont Kids, Jesus *Loves the Little Children,* Gospel Bible Songs, 2000 by Benson, Compact disc.

7. Katie Davis, *Kisses from Katie: A Story of Relentless Love and Redemption* (New York, Howard Books, 2011), 189.

CHAPTER 8

1. Katie Davis, *Kisses from Katie: A Story of Relentless Love and Redemption* (New York, Howard Books, 2011), 204.

2. Katie Davis, *Kisses from Katie: A Story of Relentless Love and Redemption* (New York, Howard Books, 2011), 214.

CHAPTER 10

1. Russell D. Moore, *Adopted for Life: The Priority of Adoption for Christian Families & Churches* (Wheaton, IL, Crossway Books, 2009), 59,116.

CHAPTER 12

1. Doris A. Landry, "More than Just the Blues," *Adoptive Families Online:* www.adoptivefamilies.com (2013).

2. Jen Hatmaker, *7: An Experimental Mutiny Against Excess* (Nashville, B&H Publishing Group, 2012), Kindle ed., 10.

EPILOGUE

1. Christy Nockels, *Waiting Here for You,* Passion – Here for You, 2001 by Six Step Records, Compact disc.

ABOUT THE AUTHOR

JENNIFER JACKSON LINCK loves to share how God answered her heart's cry to be a mother and is passionate about adoption, orphan care, and encouraging others struggling with infertility.

A graduate of the University of Oklahoma, Jennifer received a bachelor's degree in journalism and spent several years working as a reporter for *The Oklahoman*. As a ghostwriter, Jennifer completed the book *Common Threads* in 2011 with author Patty Bultman.

Jennifer is a Texan at heart but resides in Oklahoma with her husband, John, and their son, Jackson. She is unashamed of her addiction to Dr. Pepper and loves anything related to a cupcake. She blogs about her faith, family, and adoption at www.jenniferjacksonlinck.com to encourage women struggling with infertility and/or traveling the crazy, overwhelming, and expensive road to adoption. Jennifer hopes to offer a glimmer of hope to first-time mothers who aren't quite sure what they've gotten themselves into.